PROTECTING YOUR COMPANY AGAINST COMPETITIVE INTELLIGENCE

John J. McGonagle and
Carolyn M. Vella

Q

QUORUM BOOKS
Westport, Connecticut • London

Library of Congress Cataloging-in-Publication Data

McGonagle, John J.
   Protecting your company against competitive intelligence / John J.
McGonagle, Carolyn M. Vella.
      p.   cm.
   Includes bibliographical references and index.
   ISBN 1–56720–117–2 (alk. paper)
   1. Business intelligence.   2. Corporations—Security measures.
   I.   Vella, Carolyn M.   II. Title.
   HD38.7.M393   1998
   658.4'7—dc21   97–13402

British Library Cataloguing in Publication Data is available.

Library of Congress Catalog Card Number: 97–13402
ISBN: 1–56720–117–2

First published in 1998

Quorum Books, 88 Post Road West, Westport, CT 06881
An imprint of Greenwood Publishing Group, Inc.

Printed in the United States of America

The paper used in this book complies with the
Permanent Paper Standard issued by the National
Information Standards Organization (Z39.48–1984).

10   9   8   7   6   5   4   3   2   1

Copyright Acknowledgments

The authors and publisher gratefully acknowledge permission for use of the following
material:

The text of Uniform Trade Secrets Act (with 1985 amendments and official comments) are
copyrighted by the National Conference of Commissioners on Uniform State Laws, 676
North St. Clair Street, Suite 1700, Chicago, Illinois 60611. They are reprinted here with the
express written consent of the National Conference of Commissioners on Uniform State
Laws. They may not be reproduced or otherwise duplicated without their express written
consent. The authors thank the Commissioners for their kind consent in this regard.

Contents

Preface

THE CONCEPT FOR THIS BOOK

When we first came up with the concept for this book in 1995, we felt that we had the overall concept well in hand. Competitive Intelligence (CI) was already a growing and maturing discipline. We felt that the next logical stage in its development had to be on the defensive side—that is, protecting your firm from the CI efforts of your competitors.

As we have discovered during the process of writing about CI over the past ten years, writing is a combination of outlining your vision of a concept and discovering how that concept is itself growing around you. That discovery takes you to many unusual sources. As you will see, we have found examples and guidance in a widely disparate set of professional sources, including the Society of Competitive Intelligence Professionals' quarterly *Competitive Intelligence Review* and other of its publications. We found important examples and lessons in numerous other magazines, ranging from *Business Week* and *INC* to *Parade* and *InformationWeek*, and in classic books such as Washington Platt's *Strategic Intelligence Production* and Sun Tzu's *The Art of War*. Some of the more exotic sources for us ranged from wire service stories, Internet home pages, and corporate annual reports to Scott Adams's *The Dilbert Principle* and the syndicated cartoon, "On The Fastrack."

The result was that the entire structure of the book was completely redone during its development. We found that stealth competition was beginning to evolve, even without a conscious determination by those using some of its techniques that it is even there. Our vision of what stealth competition is involves cloaking your competitively sensitive information to allow you to operate as a stealth competitor. As this book developed, our vision of what stealth competition and cloaking would and should entail became blended with a growing sense of what was silently developing "out there."

THE EEA AND UTSA

As this book was coming to the end of its first draft, the U.S. Congress, after over four years of consideration, passed what is now called the Economic Espionage Act of 1996. While this act in fact dealt with foreign economic espionage, it essentially criminalized violation of the oft-overlooked state-level Uniform Trade Secrets Act. With that radical legislative change in place, we felt it necessary to include both the EEA and UTSA in our work. To educate people as to what these laws did and did not do, we have included the official texts of these laws and the official comments surrounding them.

Having done that, we found that our view of cloaking took on an additional dimension. No longer did it seem that this was a problem for a particular corporate unit to handle. Rather, as we discovered in writing our last book, what we were seeing was the development of a corporate-wide process, not merely the development of a new mission for a new (or existing) unit. We realize that it is much more difficult to convince everyone to sign onto yet another initiative, but we strongly believe that is the way to effectively cloak your business from its competitors.

MILITARY ANALOGIES AND TERMINOLOGY

You will note that we have used some terms which are derived from military concepts. Specifically, the term "stealth competitor" evokes the stealth bomber, and "cloaking" is the shorthand term used for the technology which protects the stealth bomber (as well as a concept well-known to "Trekies"). While the analogies are somewhat close, we regret having to use military-sounding terms here. After some active discussions with our fine editor, Eric Valentine, we decided that the negative overtones to the term "stealth," including sneaky, furtive, and clandestine, when coupled with the military usage of the term, made it inappropriate to use in a business book. However, we have stayed with cloaking as the operative concept, in part because it is one which has significantly less baggage.

While CI and related disciplines continue to learn much from the work of the military and civilian intelligence services around the world, all too often we have become overwhelmed with terms originating in that world. While they are now the best we have—in fact, all we have— we must always keep in mind the way these terms are used in CI, just as there is a clear difference between business competition and national warfare.[1] In one case, we win or lose a market; in the other, we are dealing with national and personal survival. While nationally sanctioned economic espionage directed at the private sector blurs this separation, for most of our readers there is still a clear demarcation.

It is with an eye to maintaining that demarcation that we have always tried to limit the excessive use such terms. In addition, for the same reasons, we felt we had to specifically disavow the use of government actions associated with classic intelligence operations, such as the affirmative use of disinformation.

STRUCTURE

Given our vision of cloaking, we have decided to take readers through the process of cloaking in several ways:

- By reminding them of how critical CI has become.
- By showing them how CI will be used to find out about them, from several perspectives.
- By explaining how a cloaking program must involve several units, ranging from CI to legal and from communications to corporate security.
- By developing general principles of an efficient cloaking program.
- By illustrating key techniques applying those principles.
- By outlining what to do once you have an effective cloaking program, as well as noting the costs of operating a cloaking program.

That, in turn, means we assume that readers are already familiar with the concepts and principles we have previously articulated about CI and related disciplines in our other books:

A New Archetype for Competitive Intelligence. Westport, Conn.: Quorum, 1996.
Outsmarting the Competition: Practical Approaches to Finding and Using Competitive Information. Naperville, Ill.: Sourcebooks, 1990.
Improved Business Planning Using Competitive Intelligence. Westport, Conn.: Quorum, 1988.
Competitive Intelligence in the Computer Age. Westport, Conn.: Quorum, 1987.

What we seek to do here is to take them one step further. We hope we have done that.

NOTE

1. For example, disinformation in the government context includes measures such as forgery. Counterintelligence also entails measures such as military assaults on opposing "spies."

PART I ────────────

THE BIG PICTURE

1

Cloaking and Competitive Intelligence

Deciding to set up and operate a cloaking program is a response to the development and importance of competitive intelligence. Thus, to understand the benefits of cloaking your competitively sensitive information, we must quickly review CI.

WHAT IS COMPETITIVE INTELLIGENCE?

Competitive intelligence is "the use of public sources to locate and develop data that is then transformed into information, generally about competitors and/or the competition." In a strictly technical sense, CI is the acquisition of publicly available data, which are then analyzed in order to produce finished intelligence about your competition. As used today, it encompasses efforts ranging from reviewing articles on the international wire services to buying satellite photographs of a factory which is still under construction.

CI is used worldwide to help firms answer questions which have previously been handled only with "hunches," "personal experience," "business instinct," or, worse, never handled at all:

- Who are our competitors—right now? Who are our potential competitors?

- Who will be leaving this market in the near future? Why?

- How do our competitors see themselves? How do they see us? Are they right or wrong?

- What are the track records of the key people at our competitors? What are their personalities? What difference do these people make in terms of how the competition will act in the future? What does their presence mean to our ability to predict how competitors will react to our competitive strategy?

- What are the short-term and long-term trends in our industry? How have our competitors responded to them in the past? How are they likely to respond to them in the future?

- What patents or technology have our competitors or potential competitors recently developed or obtained? What do those innovations or acquisitions mean to us?

- How and where are our competitors marketing their products and services? What is their rate of success?

- What new products and services will they probably be launching? Where, when, and how?

- What new markets or geographic areas will (or will not) be tapped by our competitors in the future? What current markets or geographic areas might they abandon?

- If our competitors are part of a fleet of firms, what are our competitors' parents' overall plans and goals for the next two to five years for the companies in the markets where they currently compete with us? What are their plans and goals for their other companies? How will those plans affect the way they run the companies competing with us?

CI'S GROWTH

Over the past two decades, CI has grown from a small area of interest to its cadre of founders into a discipline which is now recognized and practiced around the world. A crude barometer of its growth can be seen in the growth of SCIP, the Society of Competitive Intelligence Professionals. When SCIP was founded in 1986, its first annual meeting was attended by less than 100 people. In 1997, its worldwide membership is approaching 5,000 and growing at an estimated 30 percent per year, and its annual meeting drew over fifteen times the number at its first meeting.

Several forces have led to the widespread use of CI in the United States over the past decade. Among the most important are the following:

U.S. antitrust laws bar competitors from exchanging data in order to fix prices or divide markets. This proscription has prevented many trade associations from collecting and releasing specific information on identified companies, out of concern that such efforts could lead to prohibited activities.

Companies seeking such information in order to compete more effectively have had to develop it themselves.[1]

Competition in the United States from non-U.S.-based firms has grown substantially, and continues to grow. Over time, U.S. firms have learned that most of the more successful of these firms have been requiring their managers to collect some CI on a regular basis.

Strategic planning in companies has became more sophisticated in the 1980s and 1990s. As part of that growing sophistication, most companies now recognize that they have to know more and more about their competitors to develop a corporate business plan that will work.

On-line databases have exploded onto the business scene. Emerging from their early status as tools primarily used by librarians, lawyers, and other text-oriented researchers, these databases now enable more people to have prompt access to more raw data than ever before. Even ten years ago, most of these databases were little more than electronic indexes to articles. Now they contain everything from the full text of wire service stories and reports in local business papers to stock analysts' reports commissioned especially for on-line users. They have grown in number and in scope, with over 4,000 such bases covering the globe.

The Internet is providing another access route to on-line databases as well as to an exploding set of other resources. As more and more people begin to master the intricacies of the Internet, it is becoming a further, and invaluable, source of raw data, ranging from SEC documents to on-line catalogs and from press releases to personal homes pages about specific companies and business practices.

To their dismay, some companies already know just how devastating CI, as developed and used by both their *foreign and domestic competitors*, can be. These companies have learned only from bitter experience that to operate without CI is to operate in the dark. To compete in the dark is to face failure.

As some manufacturing and service *sectors mature*, their potential for growth has slowed. CI is rightly seen as providing them with effective ways to retain or regain market share in periods of market stagnation or even market decline.

PUBLIC INFORMATION AND CI

A key maxim of CI is that 90 percent of all information that a company needs to make critical decisions and to understand its market and competitors is already public or can be systematically developed from public data. To appreciate and fully exploit CI, you need to understand what is meant by public in this context. In CI, the term is taken in its very broadest sense. That means it is much broader than what the U.S. Environmental Protection Agency releases under the Freedom of Information Act or what you can find in the *Financial Times*. Public in CI is not the same as published; it is a significantly broader concept.

In CI, public literally means all information you can legally and ethically identify, locate, and then access. It ranges from a document released by a competitor as a part of a filing with a zoning hearing board to the text of a press release issued by your competitor's marketing agency describing its client's new product launch (while the same firm extols the virtues of the contribution to the product made by a newly refurbished plant).

Within a few years, every important recent news story, news picture, wire service report, and major press release in English (and a good percentage of those in other languages) will be commercially searchable and retrievable using a personal computer with a modem, subject only to the cost that a company is willing to incur and the time it is willing to spend. Vast amounts of other information will also be available, simply by going to "the Net."

CI AND YOUR BUSINESS

To the modern business enterprise, this growth in the use and scope of CI means that it is increasingly likely that its own activities, whether in the United States or throughout the world, are the focus of CI efforts by competitors. This is occurring whether the target is itself involved in CI.[2]

In fact, in each of the following contexts, you should always assume that your major competitors are involved with CI—at least to some degree:

- Your consumers and customers are become increasingly sophisticated and knowledgeable. Typically, they are demanding more information and openly comparing competing products, services, and sources.
- Changes now occur almost continuously in the nature and variety of the products and services you must offer just to continue to compete on the same basis.
- Significant changes are occurring in the ownership or senior management of firms in your industry, which may be followed by new operating or marketing philosophies.
- Competition is increasingly coming from firms outside your industry's traditional technological or regulatory boundaries.
- Actual and potential competition now involves firms based outside of your home country.
- The fundamental nature of competition you face is changing. For example, you see a shift from competition based on brand recognition to competition based on the product or service as a mere commodity.

Overall, CI works to help assure that competition is more vigorous and efficient, since all competitors actually know (or can know) more about each other. But that merely means that competition has reached a new level. It does not mean that there will be or should be no further changes in the form of competition now and in the future. It is one of the purposes of this book to help move competition to the next stage by helping your company to cloak itself against your competitor's CI.

In order to function while using cloaking, you should understand the basics of both CI data-collection strategies as well as key CI analytical techniques. That is the focus of Chapters 4 and 5.

NOTES

1. As an attorney has put it, "The antitrust laws are intended to promote competition between business with the result that consumers have a choice of products at the lowest practical price. The usual work of a CI professional tends to reinforce these laws. Collecting information about competitors' prices and products can enable a company to set lower prices and product better products, thus spurring competition." Dwight C. Smith III, "A Legal Perspective on the Ethics on Competitive Intelligence," *Competitive Intelligencer*, August 1989, 1, 13.

2. For help in getting involved in CI, see John J. McGonagle, Jr. and Carolyn M. Vella, *A New Archetype for Competitive Intelligence* (Westport, Conn.: Quorum Books, 1996).

2

Introduction to Cloaking:
A Case Study

Competitive intelligence professionals monitoring the Campbell Soup Company of Camden, New Jersey, undoubtedly came across what seemed to be a particularly revealing piece on that multinational food giant. In the summer of 1996, the *Philadelphia Inquirer* (headquartered just fifteen minutes from Campbell Soup's own world headquarters) ran an extensive article on the Campbell Soup Company entitled, "Campbell Soup Weighs More Cuts."[1] This piece detailed the background of an extensive corporate restructuring, which was then underway. Among the key points of that report were the following:

- Campbell Soup was "at the brink of a major restructuring that could sharply reduce its Camden headquarters staff. . . . Hundreds of the 1,500 people in the headquarters staff could face layoffs."
- Campbell Soup was "weighing the sale of some brands, including Swanson frozen foods."[2]
- Campbell Soup "may close one of its four main soup plants."
- Campbell Soup might cut its "Camden research-and-development staff."
- "Pepperidge Farm headquarters . . . could be consolidated in Camden."

This article was undoubtedly spotted by Campbell Soup's competitors. Based on that article, they should have been advising their own executives that Campbell Soup could expect a major "upheaval" in the near future. Had these firms taken action based on this conclusion, however, they would have been making a significant mistake.

In fact, what Campbell Soup Company did in the next three months was significantly different from the steps detailed in this news report:[3]

Report: Campbell Soup was "at the brink of a major restructuring that could sharply reduce its Camden headquarters staff. . . . Hundreds of the 1,500 people in the headquarters staff could face layoffs."

Action: Campbell Soup announced an elimination of 650 jobs from among its 43,000 North American employees, with 175 being eliminated at its Camden headquarters.

Report: Campbell Soup was "weighing the sale of some brands, including Swanson frozen foods."

Action: Campbell Soup decided to sell several poultry processing facilities and was reviewing "such low-margin operations as canning and pasta manufacturing," with a target of selling (unnamed) divisions representing only about $500 million (7%) in annual sales.

Report: Campbell Soup "may close one of its four main soup plants."

Action: Campbell Soup closed a Raman noodle facility in Georgia (misidentified in some later news reports as a soup plant).

Report: Campbell Soup might cut its "Camden [New Jersey] research-and-development staff."

Action: Campbell Soup announced plans to sell a poultry research facility—in Arkansas.

Report: "Pepperidge Farm headquarters [in Connecticut] . . . could be consolidated in Camden," location of Campbell Soup's World Headquarters.

Action: Campbell Soup decided to "reconfigure Pepperidge Farm biscuit operations in Lakeland, Florida." It then divided itself into two business units. One of these is Campbell International and Specialty Foods, "combining Pepperidge Farm, other bakery and confectionery brands, with frozen soups and the international grocery and food service operations."

Why did Campbell Soup's actions vary so much from the article's assertions? That occurred because, knowingly or not, Campbell Soup was operating as if it were purposefully cloaking its competitively sensitive information. That is, Campbell Soup Company was maintaining as low a profile as possible with respect to its competitors while operating in an efficient and ethical manner.

The first evidence of this lay in the article itself. While anyone reading this piece would have quickly seen that Campbell Soup was set for a major change, a very close reading of the article would have disclosed potential problems in relying on this as evidence of the immanence of such an upheaval. A close reading (and re-reading) would have disclosed that none of the sources specifically noted by the reporter for the estimates and projections of Campbell Soup's corporate actions were guaranteed to be reliable. In fact, in many places throughout the article the sources for facts, estimates, and projections were either unidentified or unidentifiable.[4] The following are examples:

Report: Campbell Soup was "at the brink of a major restructuring that could sharply reduce its Camden headquarters staff. . . . Hundreds of the 1,500 people in the headquarters staff could face layoffs."

Identified sources: Campbell Soup Company employees (unidentified in any other way) and "Wall Street analysts." In fact, one of the analysts, identified deeper in the article, noted that these layoffs might occur, but qualified this as applying only if Campbell Soup "decided to spin off brands."

Report: Campbell Soup was "weighing the sale of some brands, including Swanson frozen foods."

Identified source: Campbell Soup Company employees (unidentified in any other way).

Report: Campbell Soup "may close one of its four main soup plants."

Identified source: "Labor leaders at the company's three union plants," who all said they had "heard that one of the company's plants . . . will close."[5] The ultimate sources for the labor leaders' information was not identified in any way.

Report: Campbell Soup might cut its "Camden research-and-development staff."

Identified source: Campbell Soup Company "employees" (otherwise unidentified), who "suggest[ed]" these cuts *would* (not could) occur.

Report: "Pepperidge Farm headquarters . . . could be consolidated in Camden."

Identified source: Unnamed and unidentified Pepperidge Farm employees.

It was not until the fourth paragraph of the story that the author even noted that Campbell Soup executives "would not comment on the [restructuring] plan." And it was not until the fifth full paragraph that the story noted that the top Campbell Soup executives had "yet to make the final decisions" on the restructuring being discussed in such detail in this piece.

In contrast, a short article in *The Wall Street Journal*, which appeared one day following the *Philadelphia Inquirer* article, more accurately noted that Campbell Soup Company was only "plan[ning] staff cuts among a sweeping review" of its U.S. operations.[6] Unlike the *Philadelphia In-*

quirer article, *The Wall Street Journal* identified a "hard" source, with credibility, as its own source. That source was a copy of an internal Campbell Soup newsletter reporting on the progress of its strategic review. *The Wall Street Journal* also carefully noted that the final decisions would be made in September (the next month), but not until paragraph three of the story. However, a CI researcher accessing *The Wall Street Journal* piece would still have still been led back to the misleading the *Philadelphia Inquirer* piece, since *The Wall Street Journal* mentioned it in the next to the last paragraph.[7]

The result of both these articles was that most competitors would have been misled, even though Campbell Soup Company had done nothing wrong—it had not tried to mislead anyone. Rather, throughout this process, Campbell Soup Company had been cloaking—protecting competitively sensitive information.

How had it done that? Specifically, by doing the following:

- Campbell Soup Company declined to comment on the August 21 story in the *Philadelphia Inquirer*.

- Campbell Soup Company confirmed the contents of its newsletter to *The Wall Street Journal*, but then declined to comment on the timing or scope of the (as yet undecided) restructuring.

- Campbell Soup Company limited its discussion on future plans, such as acquisitions and marketing plans, when it announced the restructuring. In fact, one analyst was quoted was saying "You just wish there were more specifics on just how top-line growth was going to be generated. *The Wall Street Journal* noted that Campbell Soup "gave [only] sketchy outlines of its marketing plans and said only that its acquisition targets . . . will be small and most likely in foreign markets."

What operating a cloaking program means and how you can create and manage one is the subject of the balance of this book.

NOTES

1. Susan Warner, "Campbell Soup Weighs More Cuts," the *Philadelphia Inquirer*, 21 August 1996.

2. Other Campbell Soup brands, such as Godiva chocolates, were also mentioned.

3. For actions taken through November 26, 1996, see "Campbell to Cut Jobs, Close Facilities," Associated Press, in *Reading [Pennsylvania] Eagle/Times*, 6 September 1996, A7; Yumiko Ono, "Campbell Outlines Broad Reorganization," *The Wall Street Journal*, 6 September 1996, A3; Campbell Soup Company press releases, PR Newswire, 9 September 1996; Don Spatz, "Campbell Gives Different Flavor to Annual Meeting," *Reading [Pennsylvania] Eagle/Times*, 22 November 1996, B12; "Campbell Splits into 2 Primary Units," *Reading [Pennsylvania] Eagle/Times*, 26 November 1996, D6.

4. A skilled CI professional would have immediately discounted such unsupported assertions in making an analysis of the article, since the sources of the "facts" were unidentified. See Chapter 12 in John J. McGonagle, Jr. and Carolyn M. Vella, *Outsmarting the Competition: Practical Approaches to Finding and Using Competitive Information* (Naperville, Ill.: Sourcebooks, 1990). Unfortunately, too many analysts would have (erroneously) simply taken the article itself as the "source" of all of the conclusions, thus providing these conclusions with an unwarranted degree of credibility.

5. One of the U.S. plants is a nonunion plant.

6. Suein Hwang, "Campbell Soup Sees Job Cuts in Latest Plan," *The Wall Street Journal*, 22 August 1996, A3.

7. The *Philadelphia Inquirer* article was the source of several other pieces around the country on the Campbell Soup reorganization.

3

Cloaking

WHAT IS A CLOAKED COMPETITOR?

What do we mean by "cloaking" in the competitive marketplace? By that term we are seeking to evoke the image of a force that represents a real and present (competitive) threat, which has made itself virtually invisible (to CI monitoring efforts), where the invisibility is based on an understanding of the ways where it can be detected and tracked by its competitors (through their CI efforts), and where that understanding, in turn, prompts the development of strategies and tactics to minimize or even avoid detection by its (competitive) targets. Note that we have said "minimize or avoid" detection. No firm can protect all of its potentially important information. It must select what it will protect from the CI efforts of its competitors. No enterprise can be completely invisible to CI efforts. If it were so, it could not compete, for it could not be in contact with its customers, its suppliers, and so on.

Once having implemented a Cloaking Program, your firm should then seek to exploit its new competitive advantage to achieve victory in the marketplace.

WHY BECOME INVOLVED WITH CLOAKING?

Why even become involved with cloaking your competitively sensitive information? Perhaps a passing reference to the conclusions of an academic paper, published over a decade ago, can begin to bring this into focus: "A precursor to securing long-term competitive advantage is a steady stream of innovative ideas. . . . [O]ver time, the ideas on which marketing programs are based become bound to historic codes of marketing conduct. . . . As a result, the marketing strategies of competing firms converge and competitive advantage, if it is obtained at all, is often short lived. . . . "[T]he competitive environment . . . represents a potentially fruitful source of ideas for improving a firm's marketing performance."[1]

Cloaking is not the same as protecting a corporation's key assets, the job of corporate security. It is considerably broader—and very different. We will deal with that in Chapter 9. In general, however, most of those seeking to protect U.S. firms' assets, particularly their information assets, are primarily concerned with foiling industrial theft and espionage. That means they focus their efforts on preventing illegal actions, such as wire tapping, computer hacking, theft by employees, and the like. And most of these efforts are internally focused.

In terms of external threats, experts in these areas are limited to dealing with criminal or near criminal activity. For example, some corporate security experts have properly warned U.S. executives that, in some countries, "the roles of organized crime, government intelligence and banking services are all intertwined. [In those countries] organized crime uses bank information to figure out who to steal from next."[2] However, they rarely mention the broader, and legal, efforts to acquire competitively critical information through CI.[3]

Overall, your firm is not in competitive danger only from hackers and snoopers and spies. In CI, there is a fundamental axiom which takes several forms, one of which was already introduced earlier in this chapter. Basically, it holds that a highly significant percentage of all intelligence which a firm can conceivably use is available from open, legal, and ethical sources. That percentage has variously been estimated as 90 to 95 percent. The Cloaking Program seeks to protect not just 5 to 10 percent of your "information assets" from theft or misappropriation, but rather to keep as much of the other 90 to 95 percent as is possible from getting to competitors when and where they can use it.[4] This is not to say that theft does not occur. However, in many cases what is initially called theft may actually be effective CI.[5] That is why you should consider creating a Cloaking Program and then utilizing your new competitive status.

Undertaking the task of creating a Cloaking Program involves significant effort. You may ask, are you *really* putting *that much* information in the hands of your competitors? Yes. In some cases, in fact, you may even be placing it there in a nice, neat package, without the need to exert any real effort to piece it together. Take, for example, a story that appeared in our local paper in Reading, Pennsylvania. The story featured a profile of a local brick maker, owned by a British conglomerate, and included the following competitive data (and much more).[6]

- name of parent company
- annual sales
- number of employees locally and nationwide
- names and titles of key officers
- a map showing the number and locations of the three types of plants it runs
- total system manufacturing capacity, plus specific capacity numbers for particular facilities
- shipments increases—actual and planned
- number of product styles
- annual rates of improvements in production yield
- changes in scrap rates
- expansion plans

As you begin to become sensitive to protecting competitively sensitive information, your first reaction on reading an article such as this about your firm might be to shut down all external communications, such as the interviews which formed the basis of this story. That instinctive response is wrong. You must appreciate that there is a real difference between operating a Cloaking Program and becoming a hermit. If a firm has a Cloaking Program, it continues to operate in the real world, but carefully controls critical information about itself to limit timely competitor access to it. A hermit firm thinks it is accomplishing this goal by cutting off all contact with the outside. Operating in that mode can be counterproductive, causing your firm to be the focus of unwanted attention. Take, for example, the great Jell-O flap (or should it be wiggle?).

In 1996, Jell-O made national headlines when its Woburn, Massachusetts, plant was described as "top secret" and "fortress-like."[7] The Associated Press reported on this plant, which it noted refused to give tours "because what goes on in our [Kraft Food] plants we consider proprietary." That policy not only prevented a reporter from sneaking into the plant, but it resulted in the spectacle of a local politician who had been invited to the plant to speak with factory officials being taken to a small conference room—and nowhere else. State Representative Paul Casey, the politician in question, described his experience as "like entering a concentration camp."

Not all factories take such a hard line. In the equally competitive arena of pharmaceuticals, Bristol-Myers Squibb actually offers a plant tour in connection with a "Quick Changeover" workshop.[8] That is at the other extreme. The cloaked competitor operates its plants knowing how and where its competitors can penetrate to obtain sensitive intelligence. And it works to prevent, or at least delay, such efforts.

WHAT IS THE CORE OF A CLOAKING PROGRAM?

The key to understanding the concept of cloaking is to accept the fact that you can foil, to some degree, the efforts of your competitors to ascertain competitively sensitive information about your firm. Forty years ago, a thoughtful observer of governmental intelligence issues discussed the need to control what adversaries see. He observed the following:

Security restrictions are always unpopular and often onerous. In regard to any given restriction we often say: "How can this bit of information possibly help the enemy?" The answer is, "It can't, when confined to that one bit of information." But . . . this bit of almost completely harmless information, if put together with many other bits of almost completely harmless information can often help the enemy a great deal, if he is interested in the given situation and is actively collecting and interpreting such information.[9]

The key to having an effective Cloaking Program is not to shut down all data that a competitor can conceivably collect. Rather, it is to understand the channels through which a competitor collects raw data on your firm and control what goes into those channels, to determine what areas of your activities are of greatest competitive interest to a competitor and focus your efforts on protecting those areas, and to comprehend what techniques a competitor may use to analyze those data so that you deprive that competitor of the kind of data that it needs to act. From there, your firm should make sure that its employees adopt a "cloaking attitude" as the next step to accomplishing the implementation of a Cloaking Program. From that point, a Cloaking Program should be seen as a continuous screening process, by which you seek to protect your firm from the competitive intelligence efforts of your competitors. You are not managing their perceptions (or the perceptions of others); rather, you are selectively depriving them of access to critical bits of data at critical points in time.

Realistically, you cannot hope to become completely "invisible" to your competitors—at least not without cutting off all contact with your employees, your customers, your suppliers, and the public. The combination of diligent data-collection efforts in the hands of skilled analysts will enable your competitors, eventually, to determine what they need to know about what your are doing, are planning to do, and are capable of doing. However, in the real world, competitive intelligence units operate with limited assets, both in terms of time and money, so not all competitors will have conducted the optimal scope of data collection. In addition, while there are skilled competitive analysts in many competitive intelligence units, there are very few who can be considered "world-class."

This means that a Cloaking Program can be successful merely by making it difficult to collect data and develop intelligence—within time and budget constraints, by average analysts, who are probably also tracking other targets. On balance, it is not unlike one philosophy about putting better locks on your home, which holds that while a good lock will not keep out an intruder, in most cases the presence of the added difficulty will cause the intruder to turn his or her attentions elsewhere. So too with competitive intelligence—while you cannot become invisible, by making it difficult to track and analyze your efforts, you will, inevitably, cause many intelligence initiatives to be turned toward more productive targets.

PHILOSOPHY

Controlling what your competition sees is not as radical a concept as it may seem. Already, your firm may be controlling what consumers see on the news. For example, video news releases (VNRs) are an increasing phenomenon. These are promotional videos, developed for clients by professional firms, that are formatted in a broadcast news style so they can be easily integrated, either in whole or in part, into television and cable news programs. A 1996 article in *USA Today* indicated that their use was widespread and increasing. In addition, while the Radio and Television News Directors Association says that newscasters should identify these as VNRs supplied by a company, many do not do this.[10]

In the past, many major corporations had the attitude that they had invented their own particular industry segment and could never have any real competitors. Because of the pride they justifiably took in their uniqueness, they were very open to interviews and oftentimes told much more about their business than they really needed to say. This direction, along with seeing success in a new area, no doubt assisted the emergence of new competitors. As these spin-off competitors became successful, some of the major corporations continued to feel safe, perhaps even complacent, and did not see the need for any kind of competitive intelligence activity. As new competitors began to take a larger and larger share of the market, the founding companies began to waken and see that they had better not only acknowledge their competitors but also change their own ways. In a situation like this, competitive intelligence alone may not be enough. If a company has an "open mouthed" image, this must change. Cloaking must become a part of their competitive intelligence program.

BENEFITS OF A CLOAKING PROGRAM

The overall strategic goal of a Cloaking Program is to make the firm a more effective competitor. It does this by applying classic lessons of military strategy to the competitive arena. In *The Art of War*, Sun Tzu noted the following:

By discovering the enemy's dispositions and remaining invisible ourselves, we can keep our forces concentrated, while the enemy's must be divided.

Let your plans be dark and impenetrable as night, and when you move, fall like a thunderbolt.

Attack him [your enemy] where he is unprepared, appear where you are not expected.[11]

In other words, an effective competitive intelligence program, when coupled with a Cloaking Program, provides your firm with the ability to compete more effectively.

To rephrase the question, does *not* taking a cloaking attitude really make a difference? Yes it can. As an example, we can go to a highly competitive industry, quick-service restaurants, and look to the history of McDonald's, the global restaurant-franchise Goliath.

According to a company historian, the original take-out hamburger restaurant concept was developed in the 1950s by the McDonald brothers in California. But there were problems with the way the McDonald brothers exploited that concept before Ray Kroc, the founder of the McDonald's franchise system we know today, refined and applied the concepts the brothers had initiated. As a historian of McDonald's has put it,

Thanks to a poorly conceived franchising scheme, the McDonalds were belatedly realizing that an original idea that is not promoted and controlled by its creator will soon be stolen. [The McDonald] brothers were so generous in providing visitors at their store with information about their production procedures, their equipment, and their suppliers, that no one really needed a franchise to learn the McDonald's secrets. [The result was that] the brothers wound up putting more competitors in business than they did franchisees [including the predecessors of current competing chains such as Taco Bell].[12]

These few examples should help drive home the point: CI provides rewards to its practitioners. However, you do not have to make it easy for your competitors to develop critical CI on your firm. You and your company can restrict the information that others can find out about you—legally, ethically, and effectively. You do this by first developing a clear understanding of where and how CI will impact you. That is what we cover in the next part of this book. From there, you can move toward an enterprisewide goal to be able to respond to CI's advances.

COSTS OF A CLOAKING PROGRAM

You should realize that your efforts to develop a Cloaking Program will not always be met with cooperation. Information sharing is widespread, and it is widespread because it is useful. In some cases, a Cloaking Program may be considered counterproductive. For example, in the power-generation industry this trend is seen by some as impeding the free interchange of important data.

It doesn't help [predicting demand for power] that competition will discourage utilities, power marketers and others from sharing information—such as where they are suffering transmission bottlenecks; when a big customer might need extra power; or when a big generator needs to be taken out of service. Rivals could use that information to target their customers. Yet the information is crucial in an emergency, when split-second decisions must be made.[13]

While a Cloaking Program might have caused the same results, you should note that the information which the utilities are presently shielding is not the same as the data this commentator fears they will avoid sharing. The lesson is if there is a reason to share information, then share it; but if there is no reason, then ask why share it.

One area in which retailers, at least, have initiated some cloaking tactics lies in pricing. For example, Wal-Mart reportedly bars anyone from writing down prices. "The idea is to keep competitors from doing item-by-item comparisons."[14] However, these efforts backfired when they stopped a shopper (not a competitor) from doing this. Was the protection really worth the bad press?

Operating a Cloaking Program is not without costs. For example, the public company which adopts a Cloaking Program may find some reaction in the market. Take, for instance, the case of Egghead, Inc., a software retailer. According to a story in *Business Week*, Egghead had first raised funds by selling off a direct-sales unit. Two months later, the deal was completed, producing a cash position estimated at $89 million, or $5.40 per share. A month or so later, its share price was above $12. That price was based "on speculation that Egghead would do great things with the money." Three months later the price had dropped to below $8 (below book value). The reason, according to *Business Week*, was that "analysts and investors are griping that management has since clammed [sic] up, failing to enunciate a clear strategy," or, as the story lead noted, "its secrecy turned Wall Street off."[15]

There is another twist on the failure to fully communicate with the public. Another *Business Week* story (of the same date) noted that a New York hedge fund focused on investing in "companies with bad public relations."[16] These firms, the fund found, permitted it to outpace the overall market, showing a 29 percent return eight months into the year, as compared with an 11 percent increase in the Dow Jones industrial average. The fund's rationale is that these firms have "great upside potential" and are often overlooked by the balance of "the Street."

Underlying these two stories seems to be the notion that the failure to communicate with investors and, more particularly, with analysts has a negative impact on price, unrelated to the underlying value of the enterprise. The power of analysts to force corporations to disclose the information they want, when they want, was the subject of a column in *Business Week*. The columnist noted that a number of corporations time the release of critical information to satisfy the needs and schedules of large investors and analysts, to the detriment of individual investors. For example, the columnist quoted Motorola, Inc. as stating that it "report[s] our earnings at the end of the day to give our analysts time to study and absorb the information overnight."[17]

Others in the business world seem to be sensitive to the impact of companies developing a cloaking mentality. Take, for example, an editorial that recently appeared in a trade publication, in which the editor was seeking to delineate the separation of editorial from advertising:

It seems an advertiser was upset about favorable coverage we gave his competitor, while the advertiser himself got no coverage whatsoever. . . . In many cases—and in this particular instance with this particular advertiser–manufacturers and/or retailers don't want to talk for print. There will be 27 reasons why, but usually it relates to not wanting to give away trade secrets or potential market advantages. . . . I respect that, [but if] I were to persist in telling you what you already know, my publication would become irrelevant to you.

Some of you flood us with press releases. . . . We may throw 95% of these press releases away, but the other 5% get free ink on our news pages. But many of you . . . wouldn't dream of sending out a press releases, much less allow your people to talk to the media. Then you wonder why we write about your competitors so often.[18]

Does this mean that a Cloaking Program will generate problems? Perhaps, and it probably will also generate unintended consequences— every action does. But unintended does not mean adverse, merely unexpected. "Unintended consequences are not inevitably disastrous. In fact, they often are welcome."[19]

TOO MUCH CLOAKING CAN BE A PROBLEM

In operating a Cloaking Program, you can go too far. You must make sure to avoid becoming overly zealous in initiating a Cloaking Program. Such an attitude is essentially paranoid. Take, for example, the U.S. Postal Service. A 1996 report to Congress on customer service noted that business customers made up about 90 percent of postal volume. The U.S. General Accounting Office (USGAO) pointed out an almost Kafkaesque situation dealing with these customers: "An outside contractor] gathers data on the satisfaction of business customers. . . . However, the [U.S. Postal] Service has not disseminated the results within the Service or shared any results with Congress. The Service is concerned that the data might be made public if brought into the organization, thereby jeopardizing its competitive interests."[20] The USGAO dryly noted, "By not receiving any data on business customer satisfaction from the contractor, the Service and its customers are denied potential benefits for the Service using the data to improve customer service. . . . The limited release of some customer satisfaction data to Congress . . . would not seem to harm the Service's commercial interests. . . . This could be done by presenting indicators of business customer satisfaction nationally for broad customer groupings, and/or for large geographic areas."[21]

WHAT ABOUT DISINFORMATION?

Any reputable and ethical Cloaking Program does not involve disinformation.[22] As indicated, a Cloaking Program involves *protection and not deception*. Its goal is to manage and limit the perception of key elements of your competitive activities through a continuous screening process.

NOTES

1. C. Wahn Park and Daniel C. Smith, "Competitors as Sources of Innovative Marketing Strategies," Report No. 86–109 (Cambridge, Mass.: Marketing Science Institute, 1986), 16.

2. See, for example, "Tips from Top Spies," *Journal of Business Strategy*, September/October 1996, 6.

3. For a recent study of the range of such illegal efforts, see John J. Fialka, *War by Other Means: Economic Espionage in America* (New York: W. W. Norton, 1997). For a discussion covering legal and illegal efforts, see Ira Winkler, *Corporate Espionage* (Rocklin, Calif.: Prima, 1997).

4. See Chapter 10 on efforts in these areas, such as corporate security programs and the applicability of the U.S. Economic Espionage Act of 1996 and the Uniform Trade Secrets Act.

5. For example, in mid-1996, Boehringer Mannhein Corporation charged that Johnson & Johnson (J&J) "encouraged workers to illegally spy on rivals." However, the limited examples released about J&J's activities seemed to lump together the clearly illegal with the unethical (but not necessarily illegal) and perhaps with ethical and legal (but highly aggressive) intelligence collection efforts. "J&J Sued for Spying on Rival," Associated Press in *Reading [Pennsylvania] Eagle/Times*, 20 June 1996, C10; "Cloak and Dagger in the Lab," *Business Week*, 8 July 1996, 34.

6. Tony Lucia, "Glen-Gery Molding a Lasting Impression," *Reading [Pennsylvania] Eagle/Times*, 15 December 1996, C1, C4.

7. Robin Estrin, "In Woburn, There Isn't Always Room for Jell-O," *Reading [Pennsylvania] Eagle/Times*, 21 January 1996, A10–A11.

8. Productivity, Inc., "Quick Changeover Workshops," November 6–7, 1996 (promotional brochure).

9. Washington Platt, *Strategic Intelligence Production* (New York: Frederick A. Praeger, 1957), 53–54.

10. "Medialink Takes Stock in News," *USA Today*, 24 October 1996, B–2.

11. Sun Tzu, *The Art of War*, ed. James Clavell (New York: Dell, 1983), 11, 27, 32.

12. John F. Love, *McDonald's: Behind the Arches* (New York: Bantam Books, 1995), 25–27.

13. *Business Week*, 17 June 1996, 88.

14. "Wal-Mart Action Angers Shopper," Associated Press, in *Reading [Pennsylvania] Eagle/Times*, 18 October 1995, A9.

15. "Why Egghead Had a Great Fall," *Business Week*, 2 September 1996, 41.

16. "Picking Stocks with Lousy PR," *Business Week*, 2 September 1996, 84.

17. Toddi Gutner, "How to Keep the Little Guy in the Loop", *Business Week*, 29 July 1996, 32.

18. Warren Thayer, "The Indelicate Balance of Church & State," *Frozen Food Age*, March 1997, 2.

19. David Whitman, "The Law of Welcome Surprises," *U.S. News & World Report*, 30 December 1996/6 January 1997, 78.

20. U.S. General Accounting Office, *U.S. Postal Service: New Focus on Improving Service Quality and Customer Satisfaction*, GAO/GGD-96-30 (Washington, D.C.: GAO, 1995), 37.

21. Ibid., 41.

22. For more on disinformation, see Appendix A.

4

What Do Others Know about You and Where Did They Find It?

Answering this question is another step toward becoming a cloaked competitor. In fact, understanding CI data collection as it could apply to your firm is critical. Not only does a demonstration of your firm's vulnerability to CI help to convince management that the competition is in fact able to find out what you are doing, but it also helps to highlight areas where your firm is most vulnerable to the CI efforts of your competitors. That means that you can quickly identify a few places where immediate efforts will produce dramatic results while you move toward your goal: creating a Cloaking Program and then exploiting your new competitive advantage.

It is important to keep in mind the three key rules that apply to those seeking the raw data which provide the input for developing CI on your firm:

- "Public" is a broader concept than merely "published."
- When and where money moves, data move.
- Every business transaction leaves information "traces."

Thus, when you are uncertain where your competitors may be seeking and obtaining raw data on your firm, you can use these three rules as a litmus test.

Regardless of the methodology used in designing data-collection efforts, there are really only two ways that CI professionals go about collecting the data which go into preparing their intelligence estimates. First, they can visualize the raw data they are seeking as a commodity—a tangible product. Second, they can start with a list of potential resources for the raw data, and then proceed methodically through them.

Michigan State University and the Society of Competitive Intelligence Professionals interviewed government officials, university professors, security practitioners, CI consultants, and corporate CI managers. These individuals were asked to identify, based on their perceptions, the most commonly used methods for collecting information. The five most common identified were as follows:

1. hiring the competition's employees.
2. conducting pretext interviews.
3. attending trade shows and business conferences.
4. making direct contacts.
5. utilizing open-sourced data.

Additional methods, identified by less than 20 percent of the respondents, were the following:

1. lawfully acquiring a competitor's product.
2. gathering intelligence during customer or public-relations tours.
3. collecting discarded information from corporate trash containers.
4. listening to publicly held conversations.
5. conducting electronic surveillance.
6. stealing documents or presentation materials.
7. intercepting faxes or e-mail correspondence.[1]

To begin to orient you to creating a Cloaking Program, we will quickly take you through the competitive intelligence data-collection process from both perspectives.[2] We will then suggest how using defensive CI provides an alternative way for you to do this. Keep in mind that the overall goal is to help you to see where and how your competitors are able to develop intelligence on your firm (whether or not they are doing it yet). That is another step toward creating a Cloaking Program. The balance of this book will be dedicated to achieving that goal.

STARTING WITH DATA AS A COMMODITY

A useful way to approach the task of data collection in CI has been for the CI professional to visualize the data he or she is seeking as a commodity—that is, as a tangible product. When doing this, the CI professional poses the following mental questions in order to see where to focus data-collection efforts:

- Who produces the data I want?
- Where are the data I want transferred?
- Who collects the data I want?
- Who accumulates the data I want?
- Who uses the data I want?
- Who else has an interest in the data I want?

Having posed these questions, the CI professional then moves to answer them, and by so doing is actually beginning the search for the data. The objective is to identify where and when the data the CI professional seeks were created, processed, and utilized. Then the CI professional seeks to identify at which points he or she can best access elements of the data for his or her own use. From there, the professional moves to capture critical data and subject them to analysis.

Who Produces the Data I Want?

In most cases, the raw data that your competitors are seeking are company-level or even divisional-level data. That means that your firm—their target—actually produces most, if not all, of the data being sought. But your competitors' search involves further inquiry. Specifically, they will try to understand who at your firm is likely to produce these data. The key here is *generation.* For example, if the goal is to determine your marketing intentions, that raises the question whether the marketing strategy is determined by the marketing department, dictated by a strategic plan prepared by the planning department, or the result of a compromise by both units.

If the answer is that the strategy is a blend of marketing and planning department inputs, you can be sure that your competitors' competitive data research plans will reflect this. For example, when a competitor is interviewing personnel who formerly worked for you, it should be expected that they will strive to get access to personnel formerly with the appropriate departments into the interviews.

Where Are the Data I Want Transferred, Who Collects the Data I Want, and Who Accumulates the Data I Want?

The person or department your competitor identifies as occupying one or more of these situations may not be the same person who actually produces the data. The key concept here is *accumulation.* Before data are transmitted, they are usually assembled and sometimes even analyzed (or otherwise transformed), but almost always accumulated before they are moved.

That, in turn, means that one key to locating raw competitively important data is for your competitor to determine where the targeted data are moving within your enterprise so your competitor can try to intercept the data, in a figurative sense. Even a person or unit that has only had the data temporarily can be a potential target. That is because information is a "sticky" commodity—that is, a little of it stays at every place where it is handled in any way. So a person or unit which accumulates data may still retain a residue of that data.[3] That is also why the next question can produce important leads in CI research.

Who Uses the Data I Want?

To determine who uses the kind of data your competitor wants, your competitor will seek to identify persons, such as securities analysts, who seek out and then use data from companies like yours to generate company and industry forecasts. For your competitor, then, what the analyst has to offer is, first of all, his or her analysis and conclusions. However, of potentially greater importance may be the raw data—whether numeric or narrative—provided by you to that very analyst. Those data, in turn, may be disclosed in the analyst's report, may be able to be deduced from the conclusions in that report, or may be obtainable by your competitor by direct contact with the analyst.

To reach other handy repositories of such data, your competitors may be able to identify government regulatory bodies or trade associations with which you must make filings and reports or with which you file information on a voluntary basis. The type and quality of data found there will depend on why each agency collected the data in the first place.

The fact that your data are not available separately from that of others should not give you instant comfort. While entities such as the U.S. Census Bureau and private trade associations generally (but not always) release only aggregated data, as opposed to data at the company level, disaggregation techniques may enable your competitor to isolate significant data that both you and the providers of the data typically assume to be protectively masked by these aggregation efforts.

Who Else Has an Interest in the Data I Want?

To learn what other organizations and individuals may have had access to portions of these data stream, your competitor's attention will be drawn to a wide range of potential resources, ranging from the advertising departments of trade publications to academics. For example, the advertising departments of trade publications may collect or even generate data similar to that which your competitor is seeking in an effort to show that their publication represents the audience an advertiser wants to reach. To that end, its advertising department may choose to educate potential advertisers about the industry as well as about its key participants; that is, your firm.

Academics are an interesting and different resource, because their access to data is sometimes much freer than that of trade associations and the like. This may be because companies that they interview and deal with make an implicit assumption that giving academic research-ers the data is "harmless" in a competitive sense.

Of course, some firms are wise enough to insist that the academics who have access to data do not release any of the data, except in aggre-gated forms. Even when the academic is operating under such a limit, in talking with him or her your competitor may be able to discern some of the conclusions (and the bases for these conclusions) which have been drawn by someone who has already studied your company. In that case, the interview may give your competitor valuable indirect data. In addition, disaggregration techniques can work here as well as on census-type data.

Differentiating between Who Creates Data and Where You Find Data

As you focus on where the data your competitor needs might be located and then accessed, keep in mind that where your competitor eventually gets access to the data on you is not necessarily the same as the ultimate source of those data. This distinction is an important one. First, this means that your competitor may be able to access the com-petitively sensitive data it is seeking on you without ever having to contact you directly at all. Conversely, this also means that your com-petitor must ensure that it is certain whether the source it accesses for a piece of data actually produced those data or was merely transmit-ting them. If the latter is the case, analytical techniques demand that it determine the true source of those data.[4]

Confusing the producer of data with the provider of data can have important consequences to those seeking to develop CI on you. For example, just because information is available through an on-line da-tabase or from the Internet does not make it correct.

Even if the source of the data actually generates the data, more is needed. For example, cross-checking past estimates in a trade publica-tion that prints market-share estimates about an industry with the ac-tual company performance may disclose that this publication is often incorrect in its predictions. And if your competitor finds that information in a particular trade publication is consistently wrong, it may decide that it cannot rely on that publication for accurate information about your plans. But if it does not check the past record of the publication, it could be misled.

STARTING WITH SOURCES OF RAW DATA

The numerous sources listed throughout the balance of this chapter serve only as starting points for those seeking the raw data to develop CI on your firm. As the potential sources for raw data are almost endless, and they are a widely disparate group, we have divided the most often used potential sources of raw data into four basic categories: governments, specialized interests, the private sector, and the media. By grouping them, you not only have an easy way to remember them in broad terms, but, as you will see, the sources within each category tend to have common characteristics. Knowing what characteristics the data sources have in common becomes important when you analyze and evaluate how to limit your competitors' access to data on you in your Cloaking Program.

The following are common government CI data sources.

Government CI Data Sources

U.S. Government
   Regulatory Agencies
   Trade Promotion Offices
   Congressional Hearings
   Court Cases and Records
   Patents and Trademarks
   Agency and Contractor Studies—Regular and One-Time
Foreign Governments
   Regulatory Agencies
   Trade Promotion Offices
   Quasi-Government Bodies
   Regular Publications
   Patents
   Commercial Attachés
State Governments
   Regulatory Agencies
   Court Cases and Records
   Environmental Permits and Other Regulatory Filings
   Trademarks

Local Governments

    Zoning and Building Permits and Other Filings

    Court Cases and Records

    Industrial Development Authorities

As a group, government sources are generally regarded by CI professionals as providing only indirect assistance to researchers. That is because the vast bulk of the data they can access and release are aggregated, as with census reports, or are data already collected by another provider, such as information taken from a commercial directory.

However, your and your firm provide government units with significant data through channels other than ongoing broad-based data-collection efforts, such as the census. Here, we refer to areas such as licensing, regulation, and litigation files. Data collected through these channels tend to be very company or subject specific rather than aggregated. And these data tend to be relatively easily and inexpensively accessed, although it may take a relatively long time to do so.

Specialized Interest Data Sources

This group is composed of sources which collect data to advance their own specialized interests, hence the name. Those interests may be professional, or may reflect what the group's members see as a "public" or "industry" interest. The following is a list of common specialized interests that serve as good data sources for CI professionals:

Academics and Academic Resources

    Faculty

    Regular Publications, Special and One-Time Studies

    Industry Research Centers and Specialized Libraries

    Teaching Materials and Case Studies

Consumer and Advocacy Groups

    Product Tests and Comparisons

    Regular Publications

    One-Time Studies and Position Papers

Experts

    Consultants

    Expert Witnesses

    Security Analysts

Trade Associations

    Regular Publications

    Membership Directories

Special Studies and Reports
Meetings and Reprints of Speeches
Statistical Abstracts

The specialized interests all collect and provide data for a reason—to advance what they each see as their own best interests. Academics may seek funding support for research in which they are interested, advancement of their professional careers, or consulting assignments in addition to their own research interests. In these efforts, the professors and researchers may provide you with such useful input as publications, special detailed studies, and access to research centers for collecting important historical data.

Advocacy groups of all types have an "ax to grind." That is usually the advancement of the public good—as they perceive it. In doing this, they may well be spending significant time and funds to collect data, publish reports, bring lawsuits, or test products and services, all of which can provide raw data for you.

"Experts" include everyone from consultants to expert witnesses, and from clinical laboratories to security analysts. Their work reflects a common goal: to advance the individual's career, whether it is by obtaining assignments, helping an employer sell stock, or some other means.

Trade associations exist for the "good of their industry." In some industries, trade associations are unwilling or even unable to share data with nonassociation members. In other industries, the trade associations are important but little known research and resource centers whose data are available to all outsiders.[5]

The Private Sector

The private sector group includes people and organizations whose business directly involves producing or selling the kinds of data your competitor is seeking. For some, providing the data is their business. Others come across data your competitor may need as a part of their own business. The following is a list of common private sector sources of data:

Business Information Services
    Dun & Bradstreet
    Standard & Poor's
    Credit Reports
Chambers of Commerce
    Domestic
    Foreign Chambers in the United States
    U.S. Chambers Abroad

Your Competitor's Own Employees
    Sales
    Market Research
    Planning
    Engineering
    Purchasing
    Former Employees of the Target Company (Your Company)
Your Company
    Internet Home Page
    Employees
    Catalogs and Price Lists
    In-House Publications
    Press Releases and Speeches
    Advertisements and Promotional Materials
    Products
    Annual Reports
    Regulatory Filings
    Former Employees
    Other Competitors
    Customers and Suppliers
    Retailers, Distributors, and Agents
    Ad Agencies and Consultants
    Investment and Commercial Bankers

The private sector makes up the most eclectic of the four groups of information sources. In dealing with these sources, a CI professional must always avoid confusing the package and its contents.

For example, assume that your competitor has received a TRW Credit Report on a targeted company and is reviewing the data it provides on the firm's size, employees, sales, and so on. To verify the data, your competitor compares them with data obtained from another business information source, such as Dun & Bradstreet. The facts appear to be similar or even identical. To an unskilled CI professional, this provides confirmation. However, this type of confirmation does not mean really that you can assume that the original data are necessarily correct. TRW probably purchased the data your competitor was just reviewing. So if the data look the same as data from another business source, that may be because they are the same. The data may have actually come from the source with which your competitor is comparing them. That does not mean the data are correct. It is a false confirmation.

Moving to another example of private sector data sources, look at your competitor's own firm as a source for CI on your firm. Your competitor's own internal sources for data can be particularly valuable. Consider the following examples of sources of data:

- Your competitor's sales staff. Its salespeople deal daily with your customers; thus salespeople can be getting a lot of feedback about you.
- Your competitor's planning, engineering, and purchasing personnel. All of these people may be dealing with their counterparts at your firm. These relations may be through formal channels, such as associations; through indirect mechanisms, such as through common providers of goods and services; or through networks, such as common contacts within firms for which they worked before.
- Your competitor's employees who formerly worked for you. They may be hard to find, but what they have to say, if it is fairly current, may be very enlightening.
- You—the target. For example, Whirlpool Corporation now makes presentations to stock analysts featuring details such as product and service quality, brand loyalty, brand share, and trade-partner satisfaction. Traditional financial results come "second."

The Media

These varied sources all generate, collect, and process data for a specific audience. To fully understand both the data your competitor may find and how it will analyze the data, you must understand from whom the media collects those data, how, and why. The following is a summary of common media data sources:

Business Newspapers and Magazines
>   Advertisements and Want Ads
>   Articles
>   Reporters

Wire Services
>   Articles
>   Reporters

Directories and Reference Aids
Local and National Newspapers
>   Advertisements and Want Ads
>   Articles
>   Reporters
>   Obituaries

Technical Journals
>   Articles

Authors

Trade Papers and Journals; Financial Periodicals

Advertisements and Want Ads

Articles

Reporters

Marketing Studies and Media Kits

Special Issues

Related Publications

Security Analysts' Reports

Company Reports

Industry Profiles

The media, in the broadest sense, can be one of the most fruitful resources. In particular, always remember that many publications exist to serve a particular industry or market. Thus, they are positioned to help your competitor locate important data and develop leads for additional data on your firm and its operations.

What kind of help can your competitor expect from trade and industry media resources? The following list contains some examples:

- Stories, announcements, annual industry reviews, interviews, and advertisements. In short, some print the very raw data your competitor may be seeking.
- Leads—to experts, to studies and reports, to court cases, and the like.
- Secondary information on the industry that they cover. For example, advertising departments need to show that their publication is a good advertising buy. To do that, they may develop a media kit. In addition to specific information about the publication, its advertising rates, and schedules of special issues (itself an important resource), the kit may contain special studies commissioned by or paid for by the publication.

On-line Sources and the Internet

The real power of computerized data banks or the Internet lies in data gathering, and not in locating a finished, ready-to-use analysis. The key to such data gathering is to understand not only what information is being sought, but also the following:

- How the database provider or the Internet search engine being used actually searches. Are they searching titles or text, identifiers or indexing?
- How the target uses key words and concepts. Does the target use its own "shorthand," unique to it? Or does it use terms and concepts which are confusingly similar to others in the same industry?

NOTES

1. The MSU School of Criminal Justice–SCIP Project, "Intelligence Gathering Techniques," http://www.ssc.msu.edu/~cj/scip/intellsum.html (no date).

2. For more detail on this, see Chapters 6 through 11 in John J. McGonagle, Jr. and Carolyn M. Vella, *Outsmarting the Competition: Practical Approaches to Finding and Using Competitive Information* (Naperville, Ill.: Sourcebooks, 1990).

3. That retention may be physical (i.e., as file copies), or intangible, as in the recollection of someone who helped process it.

4. Realistically, many analysts skim over this step. The result is that they credit the publisher of information for the creation of the information. Thus, we often hear the lament, "Well, I read it in the [name of well-regarded publication]."

5. A trade association can also serve as a means of identifying or even gaining access to some of your employees. For instance, purchasing a trade association's membership directory may enable your competitor to find out who at your firm is responsible for the area in which it has a particular interest. In addition, attending an association's meetings may give your competitor access not only to products and promotional materials but also to your own people. Finally, trade association committee meetings can be good places for collecting raw data.

5

How Do They Figure Out
What We Are Doing?

Just as you need to understand the basics of data collection to create an effective Cloaking Program, you must also have a basic understanding of key CI analytical techniques to create this program. By knowing how the CI professional analyzes the mass of raw data to produce a finished CI estimate, you can be in a better position to develop and manage a Cloaking Program. That is because you know where to concentrate your protective efforts.

At its best, CI analysis is a difficult process. Even small impediments placed in the way of an analyst can make analysis more difficult. And foiling (or even just delaying) analysis can significantly assist you in your efforts to become a cloaked competitor. The process of analysis has three elements. These elements are (1) evaluating the accuracy of raw data, (2) applying a variety of analytical tools or models, and (3) drawing conclusions.

Through evaluation, your competitor studies the raw data as collected, eliminating unreliable or inaccurate data, falsely confirmed data, and irrelevant data. But it is only by analysis that the remaining facts are converted to usable intelligence. To conduct his or her analysis, your competitor's CI specialist will organize and assemble the useful data, sifting out disinformation or inconsistent facts. From what remains, he or she looks for patterns that reveal your strategies, while checking for omissions and displacements that mask your real intentions.

Then your competitor's CI analyst will draw inferences about your competitive moves and determine the significance of anomalies in the raw data. In conducting this analysis, your competitor's analyst may need to disaggregate your figures from industrywide reports. The analyst then has a wide variety of specific techniques to help draw critical conclusions.[1]

EVALUATING AND SCREENING DATA

Evaluating: Reliability of Source

There are four steps in evaluating the accuracy of raw basic data:

- First, the identification of the actual source of the data so the analyst can evaluate the reliability of the source.
- Second, estimation of the data's accuracy so an analyst can classify the data.
- Third, the elimination of false confirmations.
- Fourth, the determination of the relevancy of remaining data.

To conduct a good evaluation of any data, an analyst must have at least a sense of its ultimate source. That is, he or she must figure out why the data were produced, collected, and released. The origin and history of each piece of data are critical to analysis. The analyst must assume that all data are produced and released for some certain purpose. Determining that purpose as well as the source is critical to understanding exactly what the data mean. Data are only as good as their source. The data's real source (not where the data were found) should be identified before going further in analysis. Unless an analyst can establish otherwise, he or she will assume that every place from which they get data has its own point of view that permeates any data from that source.

Evaluating: Credibility of Data

Once an analyst has assessed the reliability of the data source he or she is looking at, the next step is to estimate its accuracy. This involves classifying the data actually collected as to relative degrees of accuracy. Some analysts actually use formal, systematic procedures for marking individual pieces of raw data to identify both their likely accuracy and the probable credibility of their sources.[2] The most common systems is to use a two-character classification system, such as that shown in Table 5.1

When an analyst evaluates the reliability of a source of data, he or she considers both the original source of the data (source) and the source from which he or she actually obtained the data (provider). For example, raw data obtained from your firm's current distributors may or may not be reliable. Reliability depends on the attitude of the particular distributors toward you, their supplier, their view of the use to which the information they are giving to your competitor may eventually be put, and their access to current data of the sort your competitor is trying to get from them.

There are some general conventions used by CI analysts in using this system. For example, if the source of the data is friendly (that is, one not seen as hostile to your interests) and is also an informed one, an analyst can usually assign an A rating when that source of data is known to have a long and extensive background with the type of data

Table 5.1
Data Classification System

Reliability of the Source	Approximate Truthfulness or Accuracy of Past Data (Percentage)
A. Completely Reliable	100
B. Usually Reliable	80
C. Fairly Reliable	60
D. Not Usually Reliable	40
E. Unreliable	20
F. Reliability Cannot Be Estimated	50

Accuracy of Data	Probability of Accuracy (Percentage)
1. Confirmed by Other Reliable Sources	100
2. Probably Accurate	80
3. Possibly Accurate	60
4. Of Doubtful Accuracy	40
5. Improbable	20
6. Accuracy Cannot Be Estimated	50

reported. An analyst will assign the rating B to friendly, informed sources that lack the background experience but are of known integrity. On the other hand, the analyst will assign a rating of F when there is no adequate basis for estimating the reliability of the source. This might include, for example, information that has accidentally come into the analyst's possession but that does not have a clear source, so the analyst cannot evaluate the source's track record at all.

If an analyst gets data from a source that is regularly collecting this type of data—whether it be a business information firm such as Standard & Poor's, a market research department in his or her own firm, or a CI firm—the analyst would rate the data based on two factors. First, rate the source based on its current state of training and experience. Second, rate the source that generated the data in the first instance.

There are other classifying conventions used to help manage data. For example, when an analyst has given the source of a piece of data and the collecting unit different evaluations, the analyst would then give the lower rating of reliability to the data that came through both of them.

When seeking to confirm data, there are also some conventions which reflect years of experience. If an analyst can say with certainty that reported data originated from a source other than the one that already provided the data being confirmed, then the data can be classified as "confirmed by other sources" and rated 1. If, as an analyst applies the same test, there is no reason to suspect that the confirming data come from the same source as the data being confirmed, then the data can be considered as "probably true" and given a rating of 2. If investigation discloses that raw data for which an analyst has no confirming data are consistent with the behavior of the target, the data received are "possibly true" and rated 3. An analyst should classify as "doubtful," with a rating of 4, reported but unconfirmed data, the contents of which contradict estimated or known behavior of the target, as long as those data cannot be disproved by available data. Reported data, unconfirmed by other available data and contradicting experience, are classified as "improbable" and given a rating of 5. The same classification would be given to reported data which contradict existing data already rated 1 or 2. Finally, if research discloses no basis for allocating any of the ratings of 1 through 5, the reported data should always be classified as 6, because the analyst cannot judge the data's truth.

An analyst's or company's experience with a source for data is also relevant. For example, the past track record of a source for data is generally a good basis on which to estimate current reliability. A supplemental test for reliability involves determining whether, under the conditions facing the specific source, that source could have actually obtained the specific data within the limitations of time, access, and financing that the source faces.

Always keep in mind that, under this system of classification, the ratings of accuracy and reliability are independent of each other. For example, a highly reliable source may report data which, when compared with other data that an analyst knows to be true, appear to be improbable. Its evaluation would be A5. On the other hand, an evaluation of E1 could be given to data from a source of unknown reliability when, through confirmation from other, reliable sources, the data are determined to be of proven accuracy.

Disinformation

Because CI involves transforming raw data into a cohesive picture, a good analyst must beware of disinformation. Disinformation, discussed in Appendix A, is something that looks like information but is not information.

To an analyst, being aware that disinformation really exists and trying to decide whether a competitor is providing it is a complex process. There are at least four possible options facing the analyst:

- If the analyst does not check whether disinformation is present, and it is there, it can be destructive.
- If the analyst searches for disinformation, he or she may not spot it, even when it is present. In that case, the intelligence analysis is affected by the disinformation, but in a direction and to a degree the analyst cannot appreciate.
- An analyst may spot something which he or she thinks is disinformation when it is not really present. In that case, the analyst would simply become more suspicious about the credibility assigned to what is really accurate data and more reluctant to rely on that data without further confirmation.
- The analyst may be correct in spotting the disinformation. In that case, handling it properly permits the analyst to avoid its damaging effect on the final analysis.

Precision

An analyst must be extremely careful to assure that he or she understands exactly what has been said—and what has not. Increasingly, many businesses and even industries use what is almost their own private language. Sometimes this provides clarity and precision for those who use data. In other cases, it only serves to keep outsiders from understanding what is actually going on.

Assessing the Consistency of Data

Merely because the analyst now has consistent data does not mean that he or she can immediately draw a conclusion based on those data.

The analyst will soon find out that when research seems to provide consistent estimates, it can actually mean one of several things:

- The data and associated conclusions really are valid.
- No one ever questions this "revealed truth" in an industry.
- All the data have a common source, so there is no real confirmation, merely a false confirmation.

In evaluating consistency or dealing with possible inconsistencies, one of the easiest mistakes to make is to confuse similar terms that are really used to mean widely differing things. An analyst can avoid this by paying careful attention to definitions.

Noting Patterns

While an analyst always starts by looking for direct indications of what he or she is seeking, in practice the analyst should not really expect to find such directness. What an analyst generally finds are data that involve only indirect hints. In that case, it is important to identify patterns and determine their significance. For example, reading the annual report of a corporation for one year may disclose that a particular operation is a separate division. But reading these reports covering a period of years might reveal that the prominence with which the results of that division are reported has changed radically. This may, in turn, reflect a change in the relative importance of that division to the parent corporation.

An analyst sometimes thinks of it as a corporate form of what is sometimes called "Kremlinology." Kremlinology is the science (or art) of watching who stands where on the May Day reviewing stand in Red Square in Russia, and then comparing the lineup with the previous year. From that, intelligence analysts have often been able to draw accurate conclusions about the political futures of key Russian bureaucrats and politicians.

Finding and Handling Omissions

The presence of a gap in raw data after an analyst has finished his or her research can often be as significant as what is present. For example, an analyst may find that a competitor is planning to sell a particular manufacturing operation. From the analyst's own experience, he or she may have found that this operation is a highly profitable one. If the analyst can find no reason for the proposed sale, he or she should consider that a significant omission.

A good analyst will then try to establish what the most plausible reasons might be for this action. In this example, there may be two: a possible need by the parent company for cash for its other operations or a technological breakthrough by a competitor that might make this operation less profitable or even obsolete. To determine which reason is more likely, an analyst will evaluate and analyze other information about this competitor. That could mean studying the financial results of the target's other operations and checking for new patents granted or personnel changes signaling changes in research or manufacturing operations.

Eliminating False Confirmations

A false confirmation is a situation in which one source appears to confirm data obtained from another source. In fact, there is no confirmation (or the data are disproved), because the first source may have obtained its data from the second source, or they both may have received the data from a third source, unknown to the analyst.

Determining Whether All the Data Are Relevant

It is almost always the situation in CI collection that large amounts of valuable raw data are brought in by an effective collection effort. However, typically, these same collection efforts create large amounts of "good" data that are not directly relevant to the assignment. The analyst must eliminate the raw data that are not relevant to his or her CI task. Drawing an analogy from communications, a good analyst must avoid drowning out the crucial data with the "noise" generated by irrelevant data.[3]

APPLICATION OF ANALYTICAL TOOLS AND MODELS

The Basics

How does an analyst analyze the raw data once he or she has identified which are reliable and which are not? It is like any other analysis—legal, financial, or medical. The analyst begins work knowing that he or she may lack complete data. Analyzing the results of CI is a different process for each project because the analysis used is a function of the task, the data collected, the audience for which it is being done, and the analyst's own experience.

Assembling the Data

Manipulating and structuring search results enables the good analyst to put together seemingly isolated pieces of data and achieve an unexpected result.

Outlines and Templates. How do analysts assemble data to help produce their analysis? One way is to use an outline. The outline format is particularly easy to handle if the analyst is using a word processor. First, the analyst will create an outline of the topic being analyzed. Then, as the analyst reviews the raw data, he or she inserts each piece of data as many times as needed under every appropriate heading. This is done for all the raw data. Then, the analyst will read it, section by section, seeking out what conclusions can be drawn, what problems are present, and what gaps still exist.

Data versus Conclusions. Another technique is to separate data from the analyst's conclusions. In fact, when some analysts have finished a draft report, they will go through it with a highlighter and mark data in one color and conclusions drawn from those data in another. Then, they go back through it and make sure that they have enough data to support each of the conclusions. If they do not, they either add the supporting data that was not included in the right place or drop the conclusion as unsupported. This process requires that the analyst verify that he or she has drawn conclusions from all data assembled, as well as that all conclusions are supported by some data.

SPECIFIC ANALYTICAL TOOLS AND TECHNIQUES

Forecasting

One of the most important things that an analyst can do is assist in estimating what a competitor will do, as opposed to what it has done. This *forecasting* is particularly difficult, but if done well, it is particularly valuable.

For the analyst, forecasting involves several critical steps, including the following three:

- Obtain adequate data. Adequacy is measured in terms of sufficient coverage, reliability, and precision.
- Identify and develop a set of assumptions on which to operate.
- Understand the culture of the target.

The analyst will then apply the general principles of one of two types of forecasting. *Cause-and-effect forecasting* is based on an evaluation of the underlying causes of the actions being targeted. It includes both positive causes and negative causes, as well as forces that could have prevented the action. Thus, by understanding the actual workings of the situation at present, and the causes of success and failure, the analyst becomes focused on key factors and can then obtain a clearer picture of the probability that the target will respond to a particular cause with an predicted response.

In *analogy forecasting*, an analyst seeks to understand what may happen, not from underlying trends or from direct causes, but rather by an evaluation of what has occurred in similar situations which are more familiar than the current problem. It is more appealing than an analysis from cause-and-effect forecasting, since one can often find situations which are, at least superficially, similar. It is likely to be less reliable than an analysis from cause-and-effect forecasting, however.

Forecasting improves in proportion with the amount and currency of the data being reviewed. As the activities being forecast move closer to the time the forecast is being made, the forecast should become more accurate.[4]

Fractal Management Analysis

A fractal is a particular, well-defined, easily repeated set of rules. According to the mathematician who first wrote about dimensional geometry and defined the word fractal, the degree of regularity or irregularity of a pattern remains constant over different scales.

Essentially, if an analyst looks at the whole, he or she is seeing what each small segment will look like and when he or she looks at a small segment, the analyst is seeing a miniaturized version of the whole. In that sense, fractals are not exact duplicates—they are patterns only.

One of the best-known examples of a fractal is that of the mountain. If you look at a mountain from a distance, you will see the shape of the mountain. If you look at the peak of that same mountain, you will see the shape of the entire mountain in a smaller version. If you take a sample of the mountain and look at it under a microscope, you will see the shape of the mountain approximated in that sample.

In the context of competitive analysis, fractal analysis has its greatest benefits when an analyst finds he or she must segregate portions of a target company to complete a thorough analysis. Since companies tend to function under a predetermined set of management guidelines as determined at the top levels, a predictive analysis of a segment of the company cannot really be complete without determining what these management guidelines are. Conversely, when an analyst is having a problem determining the goals and direction of the company itself, an analysis of a segment of the company may give the analyst the invaluable information needed. In essence, the analyst is assuming that each segment of a company is a fractal of the whole and then basing his or her analysis on that. When an analyst uses fractal analysis, he or she must test it, retest it, and test it once again. Fractals will not be found everywhere.

Disaggregation

As indicated earlier, an analyst may only be able to obtain aggregated intelligence data. If an analyst can derive estimates of some of the components, however, he or she can then eliminate them and draw closer to having facts about just the target. Even if partially disaggregated data is not conclusive, it may serve to confirm an apparently unsupportable estimate obtained from another source.

In one case, intelligence research located a Ph.D. thesis that had been written based on confidential data. The data were aggregated to conceal company-specific information. Other data had also been published, by a U.S. government department, but those data were aggregated in a different manner. By studying each set of data and using other sources of specific data, estimates of company-level data could be generated by disaggregation.

In addition, if an analyst cannot find out about the aspects of a business in which he or she is interested, the analyst will "step back" to look at the entire operation. Then, the analyst will eliminate all data dealing with areas in which he or she has no interest. What is left may be indistinct, but it shows an analyst the outlines of what he or she seeks. This is also a form of disaggregation. As an example, assume that the analyst cannot determine what a competitor is spending on new research facilities. If the analyst can find out its total financial picture, and then eliminate expenditures for nonresearch facilities, he or she has a good start. What is left sets the outer bounds of the target's spending on research.

Charting or Mapping

Charting or mapping is a process whereby an analyst takes data on one or more targets and coverts the data to a graphic form. By doing this, the analyst hopes to bring out existing relationships or patterns which are overwhelmed by the raw data which have been collected. The key to charting and mapping is to assure that all the raw data being charted are both complete and consistent. In particular, the careful analyst will make sure that all the targets are using exactly the same bases for language (or metrics), whether they are technical terms, measurements (of profitability, etc.), dates and time lines, and so on. Also, it is critical to this type of analysis that the process be conducted in search of meaningful (i.e., cause-and-effect) relationships.

Content or Textual Analysis

Content or textual analysis is somewhat similar to charting, in that it is a technique used to draw out inferences from an overwhelming mass of data. In textual or context analysis, the analyst searches for key words (e.g., ones that are linked to key concepts, events, or strategies).[5] The analyst then seeks to track the use of these terms, to determine, for example, the spread of a particular technology or strategy throughout an organization, or from one firm to another.

Key to success in this process is the selection of easily identified words (or concepts) which can be tracked by a computer. Trade names or unique descriptors are the best to use. The use of words widely used in the industry (such as "Windows" in personal computers) as targets makes the analysis extremely difficult to carry out. The use of synonyms for identified words in targeted documents is often a basic cause for the failure of this type of analysis, since the search design often overlooks these.

Modeling/Scenarios/Shadowing/War Gaming

In all of these cases, the CI analyst must first build up a very complete picture (profile) of the target (or targets). That profile typically includes not only information on assets and products, but also on less precise topics, such as intentions and history. The goal is to enable the analyst to prepare a "what-if" analysis of a target and its probable responses to current situations or to situations that have not yet occurred. That, in turn, allows the analyst's own firm to try out alternative competitive or even economic scenarios to determine how a competitive target might respond. Then, the analyst's firm can make its own plans accordingly. Critical to the inputs is that the analyst have a deep understanding of not only the target, but also of subjective areas such as its "culture" and the target's view of the competitive world.

DRAWING CONCLUSIONS

Checking for Anomalies

An anomaly is when data do not fit. It is usually an indication that an analyst's working assumptions are wrong or that an unknown factor is affecting results. An analyst must seek out anomalies and then figure out why they occurred. That means that something out of the ordinary should not be automatically rejected as an aberration or even a mistake. It may just be an anomaly.

If an analyst spots an anomaly, he or she must first ensure that it is not actually a mistake in the way the data were presented or collected, such as transposed numbers or a misquotation. If it is not a mistake in that sense, the analyst then looks for other data that indicate that this is something which is now true or could be true in the future. What the analyst is doing is actually attacking his or her assumptions by using the anomaly to test them. The existence of an anomaly may indicate that an analyst's basic assumptions about what is true or what is possible are not correct.

An example of an anomaly and the potentially revealing conclusions drawn from it can be seen in a case involving some futures researchers in the 1980s. One such group is reported to have predicted significant and imminent engineering developments based on an anomalous remark by President Reagan in his 1986 State of the Union message. The anomaly in President Reagan's remark was that he was talking about developing a plane for which there was no fuel. The State of the Union address is a carefully prepared, written document reviewed by many government advisers. The researchers concluded that the remark, if it existed in the written copy of the State of the Union address, could not have been a casual slip. On that basis, the firm predicted development of a jet that would fly at fifteen times the speed of sound or faster. According to these researchers, conventional jet fuel cannot be used for aircraft flights over five times the speed of sound. That remark, coupled with information from technical journals, led them to the conclusion that a hydrogen fuel will soon be available for jet flight.

Keeping alert for anomalies has another benefit. Specifically, by doing so, the analyst is helped from falling into a common trap for those involved in handling intelligence: the predisposition to subconsciously reject a deviation from a known trend or situation until a new trend or situation has been conclusively established. As a U.S. military text on intelligence observed, "This is a predisposition which is likely to be reinforced by the experience that such an expert turns out more often to be right than wrong, just as the weatherman in many climates can be more often right than wrong if he always predicts today's weather for tomorrow. Unfortunately, the analyst who is unconsciously given to this sort of pragmatism is most likely to be wrong when it is most important to be right."[6]

Preconceptions

When involved in analyzing raw data as the final step toward producing intelligence, an analyst must be very careful about his or her own view of the world and of the particular problem which the analyst brings to the task at hand. As one management expert has described the problem, "Expectations of certain data caused smart managers to ignore facts that didn't conform to their preexisting world view. Their expectations blocked out selected information about competitors, customers, and employees, masking reality until it came crashing through the door."[7] All analysis should start with as little reference to the expected outcome as possible. Only in approaching it that way will the proper focus be kept on understanding facts.

Inferences

When the analyst is studying raw data and trying to come to a conclusion about what the data all mean, one common tool is drawing inferences. Basically, this process involves coming to a conclusion in light of both logic and the analyst's own past experiences. However, that same process also may cause an analyst to fit incoming data into his or her own preexisting beliefs or to perceive what he or she expects to be there. In other words, the analyst's own experience acts as a screen on the data as well as an aid in analyzing those data.

Just being aware of the difficulty of dealing with inferences can help an analyst avoid its problems. However, at least one observer has suggested a brief test to see whether an analyst is having a problem dealing with inferences. The analyst should ask, as each new fact comes in, which of the following is his or her reaction: "That fact *is* correct or incorrect," or "That fact *must be* correct or incorrect." If the response is the second one, the analyst may be fitting the data into preexisting beliefs rather than testing the data to see what the data really mean.[7]

When analyzing data and trying to draw a conclusion, an analyst is using inductive reasoning, not deductive reasoning. The difference between these can be seen as the following: With *deduction*, you infer the particular from the general, while with *induction*, you infer the general from the particular. The difference between these two types of reasoning is more than just words. In inductive reasoning, an analyst contends that the premises he or she uses give some support for his or her conclusion. In deductive reasoning, the analyst contends that, if the premises are correct, the conclusion must be true. Because in intelligence we do not deal with revealed truth, we use inductive reasoning.

At this point, we should already be able to see some areas where the Cloaking Program can exploit the way in which an analyst operates to protect its competitive position. Part II will give you specifics on what to do—with what information—and when.

NOTES

1. This chapter is necessarily a broad overview. For additional help in analyzing raw data, as well as information on specific analytical techniques, see the sources cited in the Bibliography.

2. These tend to be based on military systems.

3. "The major causes of all types of surprise are rigid concepts and closed perceptions. These compound the effects of noise, which make intelligence work more difficult." Michael Handel, "Avoiding Political and Technological

Surprise in the 1980's," in *Intelligence Requirements for the 1980's: Analysis and Estimates*, ed. Roy Goodson (Washington, D.C.: National Strategy Information Center, 1986), 85.

4. David Henry, "Street Talk: 'February effect,'" *USA Today*, 25 February 1997, 3B.

5. It can also be used to study the volume and complexity of text, as in Jason Zweig and John Chamberlain, "Windbag Theory," *Forbes*, 3 August 1997, 43–44. There, textual analysis validated the writers' postulate that "the chairman's verbosity [in the letter to shareholders in the annual report] increases in direct proportion to the severity of the company's [financial] problems."

6. Washington Platt, *Strategic Intelligence Production* (New York: Frederick A. Praeger, 1957), 178.

7. Eileen C. Shapiro, *How Corporate Truths become Competitive Traps* (New York: John Wiley & Sons, 1991), 54.

PART II

CREATING A CLOAKING PROGRAM

6

What Should You Protect and How Should You Protect It?

WHAT SHOULD YOU PROTECT?

As we have already noted, you cannot and should not try to protect everything as a part of your Cloaking Program. Why is that true? Foremost, you cannot possibly protect everything from being disclosed to your competitors. If you try to do so, you will impair, if not destroy, your ability to compete. Recall the example of the U.S. Postal Service, where it failed to distribute critical surveys for fear that its competitors would be able to access them, thereby actually impeding its ability to compete.[1]

Second, if you actually tried to review everything that was published, released, distributed, and said by and about your firm, you would have a never-ending task. In addition, you would have created a repressive environment, curtailed free communication by your employees, and seriously impaired your ability to respond quickly in the marketplace.

Third, you have other options for protecting certain classes of critical information. Of course, your own trade-secret program should already be protecting long-lived, highly sensitive, and competitively essential information. Other legal regimes, such as patents, copyrights, and trademarks are available to protect competitively sensitive materials and concepts which must be placed into the stream of commerce. And finally, your corporate security staff operates to protect your firm from unauthorized intrusions, as well as attempts to access computer databases, penetrate corporate facilities, and so on.[2]

So what then should you seek to protect? We suggest answering that question by applying the following criteria:

- First, protect that information that is most difficult for your competitor to develop without your tacit or active cooperation. That includes information on subjects like intentions and goals.[3]

- Second, protect competitively sensitive information only for as long as is necessary. Realize that competitive information has a "half-life." There is no real need to protect it for longer than necessary (see Table 6.1).[4]

- Third, protect competitive data that would be crucial to completing a profile on your firm. For example, if your firm is increasing its market share, there is no reason to tell your competitors (through the trade press) exactly how fast you are growing—"growing rapidly" is probably sufficient.

- Fourth, protect data that are already partially protected. By that, we mean focusing a Cloaking Program on the subject matter of information already being protected as trade secrets. For example, if your marketing plan is a trade secret, protect information from which someone could derive critical elements of that plan.

- Fifth, identify the information which is critical to your operation as a business. That will vary from case to case, but you should consider guidance from the creator of Dilbert (yes, Dilbert): "Any activity that is one level removed from your people or your product will ultimately fail or have little benefit. It won't seem like that when you're doing it, but it's a consistent pattern."[5] By this, Scott Adams means that it is these activities which are not the "core" of the business. For your Cloaking Program, focus first on protecting the core, and later, if at all, on protecting competitive data on other aspects of your business.[6]

- Sixth, review the CI you are collecting (or trying to collect) on your competitors. Establish what pieces of raw data are critical to your efforts to produce that CI analysis. Also identify those pieces of data which have been difficult, or impossible to locate. Protect those from your competitors.

- Seventh, identify the data-analysis techniques most likely to be used in your industry. Then protect those key bits of information which would be vital to completing that analysis.

HOW SHOULD YOU PROTECT IT?

As this book was being written, we came across an interesting headline: "An Increasing Number of Us Are Buying Paper Shredders."[7] This provocative title led into a piece which noted, "With increasing reports of thieves pilfering sensitive financial information from trash bins across

Table 6.1
Typical Half-Lives for CI Data

		Half Life	
Level of Data	**Time Frame**	**Minimum**	**Maximum**
Micro	Historic	2 months	12 months
	Current	1 day	3 months
	Projection	1 day	2 months
Macro	Historic	3 months	24 months
	Current	1 month	6 months
	Projection	1 month	4 months

the country, a growing number of Americans are flocking to stores . . . for household paper shredders. [According to a business machines specialist] 'People are more concerned with the privacy of their information than before.'"[8] We hope that this growing attitude means that bringing a cloaking mentality to your firm will be easy for you.

Adopting a Cloaking Attitude

The piece on shredders does raise an interesting point. Do you know whether your "trash" is secure? Do you care? One security professional has noted that "rifling garbage in an effort to cull valuable information . . . is believed to be the number one method of business and personal espionage. . . . In and of itself, stealing garbage is legal."[9]

So what should be the response of a cloaked competitor? Simply encourage your employees to destroy (shred) all papers with any sensitivity—in the office—as soon as the papers become unnecessary.[10]

Consider Taking Small First Steps

To initiate your Cloaking Program to make your firm into a cloaked competitor, you might first want to seek out easy targets for the program. What makes a data target easy? Easy targets all involve the release of data which you and your fellow employees can agree are actually doing your firm no good. Such targets might include data being released in programs which could be considered to have outlived their value or where the releases could even be seen as misleading in some way.

For example, in 1997, the semiconductor industry stopped publishing what has been called "one of Wall Street's favorite numbers." That number was the ratio of the dollar value of new orders computer chip makers received in one month to the value of the chips they have shipped and billed, known as the "book-to-bill ratio." Interestingly, while it has evidently been widely recognized that this ratio was "unreliable," this was not the reason for its elimination. Press reports actually indicated that many industry executives saw its publication as a "constant irritant" because the ratios had a "disproportionate impact" on their stock prices.[11] So, this ratio will no longer be reported by the industry trade association, and its members will no longer provide that information to the association. The new data replacing the book-to-bill ratio, incidentally, provides only historic, not future-oriented data (as the book-to-bill did). You may want to look for similar releases of data to reduce or eliminate to show management that a Cloaking Program will not "hurt."

Key Precepts for Operating a Cloaking Program

To help understand how to operate as Cloaking Program, we have developed some key concepts which succinctly set forth the key elements involved. For ease of presentation, we have divided them into three major categories with three precepts in each:

What to Do

>   Seek to control only critical information, not all information.

>   Do not tell everyone everything.

>   Continually watch for sources of CI on your firm.

How to Proceed

>   Preventing disclosure is preferable to impeding it.

>   Do not ignore simple solutions.

>   Pay attention to details.

Where to Act

>   If you cannot prevent disclosure, conceal some of it.

>   If you cannot conceal it, make it harder or more costly to acquire.

>   The top may be harder to control than the bottom.

In the following chapters, we will show how to apply these precepts to specific situations.

NOTES

1. See Chapter 2.
2. See Chapter 10.

3. "It is easier to detect large scale material developments than it is to obtain information on intentions, goals, and the like." Michael Handel, "Avoiding Political and Technological Surprise in the 1980's." In *Intelligence Requirements for the 1980's: Analysis and Estimates,* ed. Roy Goodson (Washington, D.C.: National Strategy Information Center, 1986), 94.

4. Most CI has a short half-life. This term means the period of time for which the data collected retain at least 50 percent of its accuracy and/or relevance. In general, the more detailed (micro-level) the CI, the shorter the period of time for which it is valid or useful.

5. Scott Adams, *The Dilbert Principle* (New York: HarperCollins, 1996), 316.

6. Take, for example, two of his examples: First, "If you're writing code for a new software release, that's fundamental, because you're improving the product. But if you're creating a policy about writing software then you're one level removed," and second, "If you're testing a better way to assemble a product, that's fundamental. But if you're working on a task force to develop a suggestion system then you're one level removed." Ibid.

7. "An Increasing Number of Us Are Buying Paper Shedders," Knight-Ridder Newspapers, in *Reading [Pennsylvania] Eagle/Times,* 2 September 1996, D8.

8. Ibid.

9. Ibid.

10. For more, see Chapter 10.

11. "Chips' Book-to-Bill Ratio Won't Compute," *The Washington Post* in *Reading [Pennsylvania] Eagle/Times,* 5 January 1997, C4.

7

Cloaking Precepts: What to Do

PRECEPT 1: SEEK TO CONTROL ONLY CRITICAL INFORMATION, NOT ALL INFORMATION

As a cloaking competitor, be careful not to try and cut back on all communications which seem to contain competitively sensitive information. You have to be realistic. Keeping your competitors from seeing a critical piece of data can be as effective as keeping them in the dark completely—but less costly and difficult.

New Products and Services

For example, before you launch a new product or service, your firm will very likely interview potential users, talk to distributors and retailers, and consult others in the production and distribution chain. As one business start-up consultant recognized, in discussing launching a new product or service, "Sure, there's a chance that one of them [distributors and retailers] is going to tip off your competition. But if your product is that vulnerable, maybe you shouldn't be doing it."[1]

In fact, it may be that someone in your firm actually *wants* to use the media to send a message. Remember, operating a Cloaking Program is not the same as operating with no communication. On the contrary, it requires only some control of your external communications. We think, for example, the following report, apparently disclosing a future marketing tactic, was actually designed to send a message, not only to investors, but, more important, to a competitor: "Procter & Gamble Co. [according to a company spokesman] plans to offer a two-for-one deal on [a toothpaste product] as a pre-emptive strike against [a competitor's] expected introduction of a new toothpaste that's wildly successful overseas."[2]

New Orders

There are other reasons to control, but not censor, business announcements. In the aircraft industry, for example, there are indications that announcements of new orders are carefully controlled to create the image that manufacturers are actively selling their offerings. The evident goal is to drive undecided buyers to buy with the company making the announcements; that is, to get them "on the bandwagon."

Such was the situation in England in 1996 at the International Air Fair.[3] There, Airbus and Boeing engaged in a duel of order announcements. First, Boeing announced $3.3 billion in "new" business. When pressed, Boeing acknowledged that some of the orders had been placed years earlier. Trying to cover this gaff, Boeing stated that one leasing company which placed the order had "not wanted them made public until now." Airbus, Boeing's leading competitor, then announced $3 billion in "new" business. Critics quickly charged that Airbus was playing the same game as Boeing. Some said that Airbus had even taken orders off its official books for past years and added them later "to show big, sudden increases in business" at the fair.

What Not to Say to the Press

One approach with the trade press, as well as regulators, might be to understand that you must (or may want to) report on your actions, but that your obligation to report on "softer" items, such as intentions, capabilities, and plans, is often significantly less—even nonexistent.

For example, the following shows how the capabilities and plans of a company under relatively new ownership were handled in a trade industry publication. The new owners discussed past actions (which competitors probably already knew) with specificity, while future actions and plans were kept less precise:

Parks Sausage company plans to go national with its line of precooked, heat-and-eat chitterlings and sausage products. . . . To honor Parks [the company founder], last month [co-owner Lydell] Mitchell introduced Henry Parks Special

Recipe, a five-item line of breakfast sausages. Mitchell was reluctant to disclose marketing plans, but says he has already pared down the company's 102-product selection to just 20 core products. He says the company also has improved the taste and consistency of Parks' products by returning to individual mixing of spices. . . . Parks has expanded product distribution as far west as St. Louis and as far south as Florida, and it hopes to expand nationally.[4]

Competitive Intelligence Units

You may want to consider keeping your own CI unit "out of the [information] loop" in some cases as a part of a Cloaking Program. In particular, keeping the CI unit from having access to plans for changes, such as new products, acquisitions, market changes, and the like, will not irreparably cramp its operations.

Here you have a question of balance. On the one hand, informing the CI unit of such changes allows it to more effectively scan for developments which could impact those plans, as well as those impacting your current activities. On the other hand, cloistering the CI unit from such information keeps it from accidentally revealing your intentions in its own intelligence work. In addition, such a policy allows the CI unit to talk to its own sources, such as industry reporters, and to be able to refuse to confirm rumors of, for example, new products, by saying that the unit does not know anything.[5]

PRECEPT 2: DO NOT TELL EVERYONE EVERYTHING

We all like to brag, but bragging is absolutely contrary to a Cloaking Program. And while bragging can take many seemingly minor forms, it can be very dangerous. Each instance of bragging must be located and eliminated. In addition, the attitudes which generate these potential leaks must also be dealt with.

At Your Own Firm

Take, for example, your firm's corporate offices. In one instance, one of the authors of this book visited an office. While waiting in the lobby for admission, he (and everyone else there) was treated to a series of displays and maps about the firm, its operations, and its products. Among the specifics displayed on the walls were the following:

- a U.S. map showing the location of the firm's research-and-development sites.
- an in-house company magazine, free to be taken.
- a "fact sheet" on this facility, containing information such as its overall size, as well as the number of square feet dedicated to research-and-development activities there.

Your Internal Newsletters

Thousands of U.S. corporations have some sort of internal newsletter. They may be sent to all shareholders, all employees, the sales force, just hourly employees, and even to key suppliers and customers. While much of what they contain is frankly more cheerleading than confidential, that is not exclusively the case.

Take, for example, a newsletter published by Nationwide Insurance, "The Challenger," published for its "sales and sales management" personnel. One eight-page issue contained pieces ranging from an article honoring the marketing team of the month to a table presenting "New Sales Production Through July 1996 (by %)." That table showed, at the state level, how far behind or ahead of corporate year-to-date objectives each of the following areas were: life insurance commissions, homeowners insurance sales, auto insurance sales, and commercial insurance—new premiums.[6] This newsletter is easily accessible to outsiders.[7]

One way to protect your firm from such accidental distribution of competitively sensitive information is to review the distribution of information to interested audiences, through newsletters to employees, shareholders, and the like. This review should seek to control what these publications might disclose to your competitors which they could not get elsewhere. You can meet the competing demands of your employees for information and the Cloaking Program for protection by, for example, providing competitive information in the newsletters that actually comes from noncompany sources.

For example, one international bank informed its shareholders, through a newsletter, of recognition it had received for being involved with "deals of the year." It did this by noting the specific deal, but only paraphrased the publication (which it cited by name and date) for details on the transaction. Thus, it could take credit for the transaction, but did not risk inadvertently releasing information to competitors that they did not (or could not) have access to already.[8]

However, whenever your newsletters are sent to their target audience by any means other than internal mail, your firm faces a competitive risk. That risk is that a competitor will be receiving your newsletter—directly from you. That is not as remote a possibility as it seems. Once you focus your efforts in this area you may be startled to learn that some or all of the following problems exist with respect to the distribution of your newsletters:

- Your mailing lists are not regularly checked to remove ex-employees from them.[9]

- New and old copies of your internal newsletters are placed in "quasipublic" places; that is, they are available in areas where nonemployees can see them, such as corporate waiting rooms, or posted in areas accessible to outsiders, such as in lunch rooms.[10]

- New names are added to the mailing list simply when a recipient asks. In some cases, all that is needed is for someone, anyone, to send a postcard to the publication, asking to receive it. Many businesses will automatically add that name to their mailing list. Those maintaining the lists all too often never inquire into the identity of the addressees, or even check whether they are connected with the corporation.

Censuses and Surveys

Governmental Data Collection. One of the oldest responsibilities of the U.S. government is to conduct a federal census. The origin of this process lies in the Constitution, which required an "enumeration" of the population every ten years to determine the makeup of the U.S. House of Representatives.

Today, the federal census effort is really an ongoing process, and not just a once-a-decade event. It now encompasses the decennial census of population, as well as dozens of special censuses and other surveys, covering matters ranging from education to unemployment, taken at intervals as frequently as weekly.

From the perspective of the Cloaking Program, the census process is one with which you must comply. When you must respond, the materials will clearly state that fact, and federal law protects the confidentiality of your responses. What is not generally known is that a business is not required to answer all government surveys, questionnaires, and the like. Federal law requires that agencies of the U.S. government clearly indicate whether a person or business receiving a survey or questionnaire must reply (and to cite relevant authority if they contend that you must reply).

So, when you receive a government survey requesting business information, first check it carefully to see if you must respond. If you have any question as to whether you must respond, contact the agency sending the request. If you do not have to reply, ask yourself why you should. Do you risk providing information, even indirectly, to a competitor? If so, then determine which questions you will answer.

In general, whenever you provide any unit of government with confidential or proprietary information, feel free to place a legend like "CONFIDENTIAL AND PROPRIETARY—NOT FOR DISCLOSURE OR OTHER RELEASE" on all such material. The more effective practice is to provide such sensitive materials as separate attachments and then to reference them in the survey instrument, rather than answering on the page and then marking the answer as "confidential" on that page. This process makes the likelihood of accidental disclosure somewhat more remote.

Nongovernment Data Collection. You should be concerned with responding to other, nongovernment censuses. For example, when you compare a mandated census with a voluntary one, such as from a trade association, you will not see any written notice stating that your response is required by law. Even if the responses to the private survey are to be "kept in confidence," you may not be protected from CI. Crosschecking surveys and then disaggregating the results is an effective way of piercing the veil of confidentiality. While you cannot refuse to reply to a federal census, you should consider how and whether to respond to a private survey which seems to track a federal one.[11]

"Because of the increasingly competitive nature of the utility industry, many electric and gas companies have chosen not to file a USR [American Gas Association Uniform Statistical Report] in 1995, nor do they plan to do so in the future. Additionally, many companies elected to omit segment sales and revenues from their 1995 annual reports."[12]

Regulatory Filings and Testimony

Few businesses can resist the temptation to "brag" before a congressional committee (or the like) about what they do and what they do well. That tendency means that when called on to testify before Congress, or when preparing written statements for regulatory agencies, the common tendency is to provide too much. Unless it is vital to getting your message across, limit the details which you provide in such open forums. Once competitively sensitive information is provided, it cannot be withdrawn—it becomes a part of the publicly accessible record.

Similarly, when presenting written (and oral) statements to regulators, whether it is in a rule-making or a rate hearing, most firms say too much. There is a fear that if they do not give enough information in the filing to the agency, the filing may be returned for further information, thus delaying agency permission, or it may be rejected as incomplete. So companies tend to "over file."

If you must disclose competitively sensitive data to make your case, think about protecting it before you offer it. You can do this in various ways. First, you can provide the agency with a summary and note your willingness to provide additional, confidential data. However, request that the agency keep those confidential submissions separate from the public record, and only submit them after receiving that assurance. Alternatively, you might provide the agency with a summary, referring to attachments which you can submit separately and ask to be kept apart and confidential. Mark the attachments as "confidential." In any case, you should always assume that whatever you provide, under whatever protections, may become public—eventually.

Find Out Who Is Working for You

One current trend is the creation of a new form of enterprise, the "virtual corporation." While the longevity of this initiative is still subject to question, what is not subject to question is that this form (and many other variations) must be studied for vulnerability to CI efforts by your competitors.

What do we mean by virtual corporation? One definition holds that it is an organization which "involves multiple organizations acting as a single entity. It is an organization without boundaries—between its own divisions, between organizations in similar or related fields, between an organization and its suppliers or customers, and *between an organization and its competitors.*"[13]

Instinctively, business enterprises sense that arrangements such as these carry with them hidden costs, and those hidden costs often relate to the sharing of proprietary information, particularly with those outside of the actual enterprise.[14] Yet the number and types of firms involved in arrangements ranging from outsourcing to partnering to virtual corporations continues to increase.[15]

The nationally syndicated cartoon "On The Fastrack" says it all. The boss asks about how Wendy's temporary (temp) worker is. Wendy replies "Well, today, he's at our biggest competitor." After the boss's hair stands on end, you see the temp, Art, at his new position, answering the question, "What did you do in Fastrack's computer room?" He responds, "Oh, boring stuff. Payroll, budgets, contract bids . . . Nothing you'd be interested in!"[16]

In spite of the pointed message from this cartoon, most written discussions of outsourcing planning neglect even to mention, must less discuss, the need to identify and then protect your confidential information prior to initiating the outsourcing relationship.[17] If the subject of protecting an employer's information assets is dealt with at all, it is handled by using a standard confidentiality agreement. In general, a typical corporate confidentiality agreement covers confidential, or proprietary, information given by the corporation to the consultant.[18] Most of these tell the recipient, a consultant, or the like, that they cannot disclose this to third parties. What makes them difficult to enforce is that the recipient often has no idea of what the corporation regards as confidential. To protect yourself, make it clear to the consultant (as well as your own employees) what is regarded as confidential. Here, a rubber stamp placing "confidential" on documents can help.

The issue of confidentiality of competitively sensitive data does not stop there. Some consultants insist that information owned by them and flowing from them to the corporation be similarly protected. That is a fair exchange. But even when the issue of confidentiality is dealt with as noted, there is still a significant gap. What is missing is coverage of information or even raw data that the consultant generates for the benefit of its corporate client. These data have not yet been in the possession of the corporation, so the corporation's confidentiality clause does not cover it; it is not exclusively the property of the consultant, so the other does not cover it either. What is often lacking is contractual coverage of confidential or sensitive data, work, and so on performed or collected by the consultant for the client. The consultant should be under a duty to treat that as confidential in the same way it would data provided by the client.

Communications with Nonbusiness Publications

Limiting the contents of announcements should not be limited to what your firm says in trade publications. You should make your employees aware of the need to control information which is both personal and corporate. For example, university alumni magazines are a sporadic, but sometimes useful, source of information on corporate changes. This information comes to light from the desire of your employees to brag to their former classmates. In so doing, they risk disclosing information not available elsewhere.

A very dated example of how effective researchers can access otherwise inaccessible information may drive this point home. In the 1960s, *Time* magazine was still dominated by its founder, Henry Luce. Luce was generally regarded as a very difficult man to contact. However, a group of students at his alma mater, Yale University, had no difficulty in talking to him at his home about speaking at a campus event. His unlisted telephone number and residence address were published in the Yale University Alumni Directory.

Incoming Cold Calls

Teach your employees to *listen* when they are on the telephone with someone with whom they are not familiar. They should understand that politeness does not require that they respond to every question. Consider this methodology for collecting CI: "Wolf Co. wants information about a competitor—Sheep Co. [An outside CI firm] begins with a database search. To fill in the blanks after that, she sometimes calls Sheep Co. directly and asks lower-level employees specific questions about prices and products, blending sensitive questions into what might sound like a harmless market survey."[19]

Trade Shows, Interviews, and Meetings

Some firms make extensive use of trade shows, conferences, and other meetings as primary sources of raw data for their CI. They attend these meetings because they are seen as resources for gaining data from the attendees as well as from the presentations. This is, of course, proper and legitimate.

However, there have been techniques used in connection with such shows, as well as in other contexts, which are questionable and should cause concern. Some of the most frequent questionable tactics include the following:

- Phantom interviews are when a potential employer, a competitor, talks with your key personnel under the guise of filling a vacancy which does not exist. The goal is to obtain information through your employee's understandable efforts to explain what he or she does in the best possible light.

- False-flag job seekers are the converse of the phantom interview. A trusted employee of a competitor approaches your firm seeking employment. The goal is to use the employment and interview process to learn about your firm. The employee has no real interest in any job change.

- Seductions are when one of your own employees is encouraged to talk about how important or technically proficient he or she is—by flattery. The means can include discussing a third party's products, indicating confusion over a new technical development, or even challenging a professional's knowledge. The goal is to elicit key data about your business.

- A no-sale sale is when a competitor talks with your distributors, vendors, or licensees. These firms are led to believe they are being courted to carry your competitor's line of goods or services. This may be true, but if it is, there is an additional, hidden agenda. They are also being pumped for hard information on such topics as your prices.

As with all aspects of managing a Cloaking Program, do not overreact. Do not immediately avoid industry and technical meetings because of a fear that your competitors might turn them into an opportunity for CI. The benefits of attending are substantial, and following a few simple rules should prevent major damage. Remember, failing to attend these functions does not prevent your competitors from accumulating information about your business as much as it may cut you off from information about them.

Thus, to be able to benefit from these meeting and other functions while feeling comfortable about limiting the amount of CI that can be developed about your firm, consider the following tips:[20]

- Executives and supervisors should not disclose anything to employees that they do not want competitors to know about without at least warning the employees about it. For example, a number of years ago, it was reported that an employee of a major express package company accidentally disclosed the company's plans to expand to Europe. The disclosure came during a discussion at a training meeting attended by representatives of a major competitor. These plans had not been made public.

- Do not take any sensitive materials with you to a meeting, even to work on in your hotel room. They could end up in the wrong room, or they could be accidentally distributed, destroyed, or duplicated.

- Check in advance what will be given out at the conference or meeting by your firm and its employees. If possible, have someone not in the department involved with preparing and distributing the materials check them. For example, materials such as media kits may disclose or hint at data which people in research and development, for example, do not want in the public domain.

- Brief key employees on what to say about critical issues or topics. Do you want certain things disclosed, or is no comment the right answer?

- Modify routine written materials distributed in connection with meetings and travel, such as expense record-keeping packages or instructions on entertaining, to include at least a cautionary message about exercising care with competitively sensitive information.

You can also give your employees guidance on how to deal with the traps noted. If an employee suspects a phantom interview, he or she may be able to smoke it out, without losing the chance for a legitimate position, by asking the following questions: Who is the supervisor? Do you have a copy of the job description? What sort of work would be involved? Who is doing the job now? Why is the position vacant, or being added? Typically, the answers to these will be evasive if the interview is just a ploy for gathering CI.

With respect to false-flag job seekers, remember, above all, any persons interviewing with you are not bound to protect your trade secrets because they do not work for you. Be careful if the interview seems to be directed to discussions about the future position and the work you are doing now and will be doing in the future, and away from the individual and the individual's experience and qualifications. Be aware if the interviewee's questions shift from those about the position to specific questions about other areas of the firm's activities. Watch out for indications that a facility visit is being sought. For highly sensitive positions, you may even want to consider preparing a nondisclosure agreement covering information disclosed in the interview process.

If the ploy is a seduction, all you can do is warn employees to use their common sense. Remind them that very few people are really that interested in exactly what they do for a living. Little can be done to keep outsiders from initiating no-sale sales except to warn the firms with which you have the closest relationships that disclosures about your business may hurt their favored position with your firm.

PRECEPT 3: CONTINUALLY WATCH FOR SOURCES OF CI ON YOUR FIRM

You should try to think through where your competitors would go to find CI on your firm—and then monitor what those sources reveal.[21] This search for new sources that your competitor might exploit should be an ongoing process.

Database Searches

What is available on databases is really a function of what you file with government agencies, such as the SEC, as well as what you put (or permit to be placed) in the trade and business press. By operating a Cloaking Program, you reduce the foot print your firm leaves for the experienced database searcher to follow. What you should be trying to do is to make the task at least as difficult as it would be for a search on a private company (or to make it more difficult if you are already private). Take heed of what these searchers are told about developing company profiles: "Researchers tracking private companies usually must cross-check facts from multiple sources. This can substantially expand the search process and require using expensive business information services, and often yields less complete information in the end."[22]

This means that one way to make searches more difficult is to avoid using words or phrases which are often sought and easily captured by automated filters. These are words and concepts such as "merge," "discover," "capacity," or "new product." It may be somewhat difficult to keep them from your filings and press releases, but if it can be done, it makes classification and ultimately recovery of data more difficult. In addition, when you make public filings, see if you can file under a name not well-known to the competition. For example, perhaps your EPA filings could be made by MECC Inc. (for My Environmental Compliance Corporation, Inc.) rather than by your well-known public identity. Check into it.

Watch Out for the Non-Obvious

When monitoring where and when trade information on your firm emerges, do not restrict yourself to the most obvious areas, such as general business publications (e.g., *Business Week*) and trade publications covering your specific industry. In addition to checking these, always check out local newspapers, covering not only your headquarters area, but also those local papers serving the areas around your plants and other key facilities; local business newspapers, covering both headquarters and, more important, the headquarters of separate business units as well as the locations of major facilities; and transindustry publications, which deal with subjects ranging from information technology to business travel.

Publications in the first two categories can be profitable sources of data, even if it does not originate with you. Take, for example, the content of statements issued by a lawyer for Pennsylvania beer brewer D. G. Yuengling & Sons, Inc. That brewer was engaged in a year-long search for a site for a new brewery. That site search had been well covered by the local press in Pennsylvania, since a new brewery would mean a significant number of new local jobs with the nation's oldest operating brewer. So Yuengling, having discussed its search with the press over time, obviously felt obliged to indicate that the search had been concluded. However, while making known the fact that the firm would not build a new brewery, Yuengling also stated that it was preparing to meet increasing demand for one product, Yuengling's Black and Tan, by contracting for its production with Stroh's Brewery (a competitor) in a nearby Pennsylvania county.[23]

It is publications in the last category, transindustry, which often can be surprisingly open and detailed in discussing your business. This is for several reasons. The audience served by these publications are usually interested in very technical, cutting-edge, and current reports, so the publications will not print very general pieces. The audience also often needs background on the subject of the piece—that is, the company—rather than on the technical matters covered by the piece, so a reporter may put a significant amount of effort into "setting the stage," providing in-depth data on your firm and the competitive environment. These pieces are often based not just on information provided by your firm, but also rely on information provided by informed third parties, such as consultants, contractors, and the like.

Take, for example, an article that appeared in *InformationWeek*. This article profiled how General Motors' Saturn division used information technology.[24] In doing so, it provided a significant amount of detailed information on the current and future technology at the plant, which would be expected.[25] However, it also offered information on the production activities at the Spring Hill, Tennessee, plant, including the following:

- Production lines are run by teams, rotating individual production tasks.
- The plant currently runs at one car per minute, with a production schedule of twenty hours a day, six days a week.

- The plant was suffering production bottlenecks.
- Ten percent of manufacturing processes have been moved from Digital Equipment VAX to a mix of Windows NT–based manufacturing packages and Microsoft applications on NT and Windows 95 with an aim to eliminate the bottlenecks.
- The installation of this manufacturing software is a part of Saturn's efforts to define its strategy into the year 2000 and beyond. That program began around 1993, which means it is using a seven-year horizon for planning.

Trading Information

Do your employees trade information with your competitors? Do not automatically answer no. The correct answer is maybe. A 1991 paper notes (ominously) that "Individual employees provide [technical] information to colleagues from other firms with the expectation of receiving valuable information in return, either immediately or in the future."[26] This analysis further postulated that such exchanges were in fact beneficial in technologically active industries and should not be discouraged. The basis is that those making the transfers did so with the reasonable expectation that they would receive equally beneficial information in return.

However, such informal exchanges should be discouraged for at least two reasons. First, the very act of making such uncontrolled transfers of competitive information is fundamentally contrary to your position as a cloaked competitor. An exception to cloaking like this type of an exchange cannot be permitted unless there is a compelling reason for it. Second, as your competitors increase their vigilance, whether through corporate security programs, trade-secrets management, or cloaking behavior of their own, the likelihood that you will receive data of value in return for each exchange should actually diminish over time. To be blunt, in such an atmosphere the exchanges will eventually diminish and then halt. As in a game of musical chairs, the last firm to transfer technical data is the loser.

NOTES

1. John Luther, quoted in "Why Not to Worry about Confidentiality," *INC.*, April 1990, 116.

2. Dow Jones News Service, "P&G Trying to Squeeze Colgate," *Reading* [Pennsylvania] *Eagle/Times*, 4 August 1996, B6.

3. "Airbus, Boeing War over Sales Claims," Associated Press, in *Reading* [Pennsylvania] *Eagle/Times*, 4 September 1996, D8; Associated Press, "Boeing Wins $1.18 Billion 747 Order," *Reading* [Pennsylvania] *Eagle/Times*, 5 September 1996, A17.

4. Arthur Goldgaber, "Pig Tales," *Food Processing*, April 1997, 39.

5. This is the policy of at least one of the "Big Three" U.S. auto makers.

6. Nationwide Insurance, *The Challenger*, August 1996.

7. Even if it were not officially available to outsiders, you should always assume that your competitors may access copies of it.

8. "Citibank Leadership," *[Citibank] CCINVESTOR*, June 1996, insert.

9. See Chapter 4.

10. It is not just newsletters that are left in waiting rooms. In one case, an employee of a major pharmaceutical firm picked up a manual on a competitor's new product "from a distributor's waiting room. It was eventually returned" to the competitor. "Cloak and Dagger in the Lab," *Business Week*, 8 July 1996, 34.

11. One layer of protection which you should inquire into is to ask who can access the entire survey results. If you cannot keep it from becoming public, perhaps you can participate only if access to the results is limited to those who contribute to it.

12. *The PUR Analysis of Investor-Owned Electric and Gas Utilities: 1996 Edition* (Vienna, Va.: Public Utilities Reports, 1996), v.

13. Sam Dickey, "Enterprises without Boundaries," *Beyond Computing*, May 1996, 21 (emphasis added).

14. Ibid., 24; "Data, Data Everywhere," *Adweek*, 10 June 1996, 44. Similar issues arise within companies as well. See, for example, Hildy DeFrisco and Mary Lang, "Installing Collaborative Behavior in Client Organizations," *Virtual Workgroups*, July / August 1996, 39–44.

15. See, for example, "Ryder Sees the Logic of Logistics," *Business Week*, 5 August 1996, 56.

16. Bill Holbrook, "On The Fastrack," 29 November 1993.

17. See, for example, "Six Steps to Outsourcing," *Beyond Computing*, March 1997, 40.

18. For more on this topic, see Chapters 8 and 10.

19. John J. Fialka, *War by Other Means* (New York: W. W. Norton, 1997), 129.

20. These same principles apply when you or your employees are dealing with outsiders in other contexts, such as over the telephone.

21. For a discussion on related organizational issues, see Chapter 10.

22. Barbara Quint, "Real Searches, Real Money," *Online User*, May / June 1996, 25–26.

23. "Plans to Build New Brewery Are Canceled by Yuengling," *Reading [Pennsylvania] Eagle/Times*, 2 August 1996, A6.

24. "Saturn Puts NT to Work," *InformationWeek*, 19 August 1996, 55–56.

25. Ibid. The bulk of this is captured in a "Technology Snapshot," listing key software, hardware, and network facilities.

26. Stephen Schrader, "Information Technology Transfer between Firms: Cooperation through Information Trading," *Research Policy* 20 (Jan. 1991): 153–170.

8

Cloaking Precepts: How to Proceed

PRECEPT 4: PREVENTING DISCLOSURE IS
PREFERABLE TO IMPEDING IT

The best way to keep data from your competitor is to keep the data from being disclosed. While other options are worthwhile to explore, security is best achieved if the competitor never has access to data, rather than if it has limited, costly, or delayed access.

Court Cases

In civil litigation today, the parties usually engage in discovery. Discovery is the process of collecting evidence from each side, outside of court but under the supervision of the court, in anticipation of trial. Both parties are, in general, obligated to give to the other side documents which are asked for. Whether these documents can, or even should, be entered into evidence at the trial is not a consideration at the discovery stage.

For that reason, during the discovery phase of litigation, your business may have to provide information to the opposing party which you would prefer to be kept confidential, but which is not strictly a trade secret.[1] Merely because you consider it confidential is not usually a good reason to refuse to provide it during discovery. If faced with the situation of having to provide sensitive information during discovery, you should consider using one or more of the following options that are available to any party to a lawsuit:

- You can have the other side sign an agreement, called a *stipulation*, which requires the other party to keep certain documents or information in confidence.
- Your attorneys can request that the judge supervising the discovery enter a protective order controlling who sees the discovery and under what circumstances. That protective order may, if approved, even have the parties put the discovery documents in a location where they are subject to inspection only, but not copying, if they are very sensitive.
- You and your attorneys should consider whether you need to prevent the opposing party and its attorney from discussing what they have seen with others. A stipulation or protective order may be needed to accomplish this.
- Make sure that when you and your attorney provide discovery that you have not automatically agreed to allow the discovery to be used in evidence. If you have, you have lost the ability to keep it out of the court record, even though you protected it during the discovery phase.
- If written interrogatories (questions calling for written answers) or depositions (testimony given before a court reporter and transcribed) are being used during discovery, have both sides agree (in advance) not to file the results with the court. That is because once they are filed, they become a part of the permanent record of the case, and anyone can access them simply by calling for the file at the courthouse and paying for copies.

Keep in mind that once a trial has begun, everything that is introduced as evidence and all the transcripts of the trial are generally (and usually automatically) a part of the public record. Anyone can pay to get copies of any (or all) of that record. While you cannot control what your opponent introduces into evidence, you can ask the court, in advance if possible, to take special measures to keep such matters in confidence—and out of the public record.

Finally, let us assume that you and the other party have settled your dispute without a judge or jury having to come to a final disposition of the matter by a trial. Do not forget about all of the discovery that has been produced through the process of the case. In settling the case, the parties can agree to return all copies of the discovery, to control (or even prevent) its distribution to third parties, and even agree not to discuss the discovery with third parties. If this protection is important, get it set out in the settlement order. If this is very critical, make sure that the terms of the settlement is actually an order of the court. That means that the terms of the disposition of the case between the parties is signed by the judge and then entered into the record of the court. If one party violates the settlement agreement, the other can go directly to the judge for relief without having to file a new lawsuit.

SEC Reports

One of the areas providing rich sources for raw data on public-traded corporations are annual reports to shareholders. Most of these reports are glossy, four-color presentations that the corporations lavish a significant amount of time and money producing. The senior officers of the corporation spend significant amounts of time in composing the messages presented by the chairman and president in these documents. These messages, as well as much of the annual report, deal with nonfinancial, and often competitively interesting, events and information. In fact, there is pressure on public companies to increase the amount of nonfinancial data which is released to the public.[2] The primary vehicle for such disclosures is (or would be) the annual report to shareholders.

What many people do not realize is that U.S. corporations do not have to prepare a report of this kind. What they do have to do is file a report with the U.S. SEC, the so-called Form 10-K. So you may want to consider limiting the optional report. Not only will you save money, but you may tighten up on ways in which your corporation's operations are disclosed to competitors. Remember, not only do your competitors read the report, they also look at all the pictures.

For an example of one way that you can control disclosures in your reports, you might consider the approach taken in 1994 by Mellon Bank Corporation. That year, the bank released what it called a "Cost-Effective Annual Report." It was printed on nonglossy, lightweight paper. As Mellon noted, "This simplified format contains the same level of information as published in previous years' traditional annual reports, including the highlights of our past year's performance, as well as complete financial statements."[3]

This document was 90 pages long. In 1995, without comment, Mellon returned to the traditional, glossy, four-color report.[4] The report then contained 102 pages of text. The additional pages represented material not present in the 1994 report, called "The Year In Review." This section stressed specific elements of Mellon's competitive activities and strategies.[5] In your Cloaking Program, you might want to consider emulating the 1994, rather than the 1995, annual report.

In 1994, Mellon had offered "limited quantities" of a full-color publication, the *Mellon Bank Corporation 1994 Annual Review*. By requiring individuals to request this item specifically, Mellon made it slightly more difficult for nonshareholders to get easy access to this supplement. However, using commercial services that access the SEC's files, any outsider could have gotten access, at least to a black and white copy of this document.

In addition, while calling it a cost-saving measure, Mellon announced it would discontinue publishing a "condensed quarterly report." It would, however, provide quarterly financial information to shareholders "upon request."[6] Here too, Mellon could control access to information generated for its shareholders.[7]

Regulatory Filings

Avail yourself of every opportunity to require (or at least request) that data which are provided to regulatory agencies or bodies for any purpose only be released or referred to by that body in an aggregated form. That is, the agency will combine the data with that of other filers, and not even make reference to the data in an unidentified way, such as "company reports show results ranging from a low of 3.578 to a high of 5.321." Even though your name is not attached to either number, it may be very easy for a competitor to attach it.

Realize, however, that aggregation, by itself, does not guarantee protection. If your data are available in different forms, even aggregated, it is still possible to disaggregate the data, under the proper circumstances.[8] However, consistently protecting the data in this and other ways make the task of dissagregation that much more difficult.

PRECEPT 5: DO NOT IGNORE SIMPLE SOLUTIONS

Too often, when initiating any new internal program, firms feel the need to initiate widespread, complex programs, presumably believing that an important problem demands a forceful response. However, there are simple steps that everyone can take which quickly reduce your profile to your competitors.

Mailing Lists

Check all your firm's mailing lists. By this, we mean all lists maintained by your firm, as well as *for* your firm by advertising agencies and the like. There are a variety of steps which you can insist be taken immediately with respect to such lists.

First, remove all terminated, retired, or transferred employees from the mailing list of employees receiving any newsletters. Then, make sure that information on price lists, new products, and the like is going only to current suppliers and distributors, and not to firms which are no longer representing your firm. Sending price and product updates to them may be like sending it directly to a competitor. From there, you should remove from the lists, at least temporarily, all recipients whom you cannot immediately identify, as well as names with questionable addresses.[9] Then send qualification cards to all of these recipients. In that way, you can identify who they are and why they should be on this list. If those being sent cards do not reply, remove them from the list.

When you send out qualifying cards, do not be shy. You should feel free to ask them if they are receiving the mailings on behalf of a competitor. If they are, then you know it and can decide whether or not you want that to continue.

Not only will a regular purging process make access by those seeking CI on your firm more difficult, it will save you money as well.

Trash

According to one industrial security consultant, rifling garbage, which is legal in many contexts, "is believed to be the number one method of business and personal espionage."[10] Yet foiling this collection effort, sometimes called "dumpster diving," requires only that you and your employees observe a few logical rules. Such rules should require the destruction of all waste paper before recycling, and the regular use of paper shredders in the office and at home, if your employees take work home.

E-mail

One of the fastest growing areas of corporate communication is e-mail. With the explosive growth in the use of e-mail have come a number of concerns to firms. For employers, these concerns range from preventing "spamming," the virtually uncontrolled remailing of messages to vast networks of recipients, to managing liability issues for "flaming," where e-mail senders vent their emotions in ways (and in words) almost unimaginable.

What underlies all this is that e-mail is now the fastest growing and least controlled form of written communication. One problem here is that there is a real legal question whether you, the employer, can monitor your employee's e-mail sent on company systems. One case, in Oklahoma, seems to hold that "employees have a right to expect that their employers will refrain from monitoring e-mail messages transmitted on company systems."[11] That means that, with a keystroke, one person can send a message around the world, or can forward something he or she has just received to someone who needs to see it now, or can send copies of an important memo to hundreds of readers. And this can be done all at once—without you, the employer, being able to intervene.

Unfortunately, it is just as easy and fast to send the wrong message to the wrong person. This situation, called "data leakage," involves one or more copies of an e-mail message being sent outside of the firm, where the e-mail inadvertently discloses confidential information.[12] That mismailing can occur either by mistyping the address or by having the message misrouted by one of the many stations involved in handling e-mail sent outside of an organization on the Internet.

One solution (and here corporate security and the Cloaking Program overlap) is to adopt a formal e-mail policy. That policy may be as a simple as this one suggested by a consultant: "State in an E-mail policy that employees should *not* include in an E-mail message anything they wouldn't be willing to say in an open business meeting: no tasteless jokes, no ethnic slurs, or prejudicial comments, and no slanderous remarks about fellow employees—or even about the competition."[13] Of course, the Cloaking Program should mandate including competitively sensitive information as well in that litany of subjects not suitable for e-mail.[14]

Your corporate security office should also be involved with related areas of e-mail management, such as protecting your own internal e-mail systems from "hackers" operating through your Internet page. That involves consideration of techniques ranging from using firewalls and multiple servers, to avoiding a direct link between a Web site and your e-mail.[15] You should also keep your internal data secure from insiders. A story from South Carolina makes this point well: "A small maker of virtual-reality games in South Carolina faced a problem. A 'disgruntled' employee quit. As a 'parting shot' the employee password-protected some documents that were vital to the firm's business. He then refused to disclose the passwords unless the company paid him off. While the software maker said that there was no way to break into the documents, the firm was able to find a programming expert, who then 'surfed the net' and located a program to decrypt these documents."[16]

Travel

The accidental release of competitively sensitive information while traveling is very common, but rarely discussed.

Public Telephones. When we travel, we are all warned to be careful with our telephone calling cards. Why? Because the numbers we use can be "skimmed" and then used to make calls charged to our account. How are they skimmed? By someone who is standing up to twenty-five feet away, watching how we dial.

But we rarely worry about having our conversations "skimmed." We are so used to the lack of privacy in telephone kiosks that we often say too much. On one recent trip, while waiting for a response on a pay telephone, the following sentence was heard: "This is what I negoti-ated. . . ." Chill your blood? It should. What are the odds that this infor-mation might be overheard by someone who could use it and who would know the subject? Not significant, but such eavesdropping is possible.[17]

Computers. The "road warrior" today is identified by his or her por-table computer, and those with computers use them—sometimes when-ever they have the chance. That can be in the airport, as well as on the airplane. Rarely, if ever, have we ever seen one of the "road warriors" turn off a computer if there was someone with a direct line of vision to the screen. But people do have a line of sight to the screen, and with improved lighting and colors, the screens are now visible further and further away. Would you allow your employees to turn on their computers and work while they were in the lobby of a competitor? No, but most firms al-low, if not encourage, such work while the employee is airborne. Re-member, you do not know who is nearby—or whom they work for.

Faxes. When you are traveling, you may find that you want to send or receive a fax that contains important information. Should you worry about protecting your firm? Outgoing faxes are not likely to fall into the hands of a competitor—or are they? That depends on how you handle them. Do you take them down to the business center and wait while they are faxed? This involves no risk. Do you leave them in the in box? This is not a good idea. Do you call room service and put it into their hands? That is the riskiest scenario, not because the hotel person-nel will do something wrong, but because you have increased the num-ber of times the material is transferred, and each transfer has its own risk. If you are sending from a hotel, the original might go back to the wrong room. This could be a problem. If you are at a trade association meeting or convention, where the odds of a mistake being costly in-crease—rapidly.

What about incoming faxes? If you must do it via the hotel (and cannot use your own PC or another secure option), try and have the sender send the materials at a specific time. Then arrange to be at the business center at that time to get the materials, without anyone else handling them.

Cellular Telephones. Whether you are talking on a mobile telephone in your car or on the plane or even on a portable telephone at home, always assume that someone else is listening. Speak in general terms and make everything you say sound uninteresting. As a security ex-pert recently noted, "Cellular and cordless telephones are among the easiest of eavesdropping targets. Contrary to common perception, re-ception of these conversations is generally crystal clear. [Monitoring this] transmission is illegal. Do not rely on the laws to protect your privacy, though. They are generally considered unenforceable."[18]

Another expert suggests adopting very simple precautions when using any cellular service, including the following:

Assume that someone is always listening.
Be as vague and uninteresting as possible.
Use first names only.
Do not use company names.[19]

Take Advantage of What Is Offered

As companies become concerned about their employees disclosing critical materials at conferences and trade shows, some of the sponsors of these functions have responded. Take, for example, an advertisement for a workshop on "total productive maintenance." The workshop attendees, according to the sponsors, were expected to discuss their own operations in some depth during the course of the meeting. For that reason, it seems, the sponsors noted in the workshop materials that "Competitive Companies May Not Be Allowed To Attend This Event."[20] If your firm was planning to attend, you might want to insist that this pledge be honored.

PRECEPT 6: PAY ATTENTION TO DETAILS

Sometimes you can operate an effective Cloaking Program, protecting critical competitive information, simply by paying attention to what seem to be relatively minor details. Attention to some of these details could serve to thwart or even throttle CI efforts against you.

Check Regularly Produced Documents

If you create public documents, such as annual reports or catalogs, on a periodic basis, you (or your staff) typically start with the document to be superseded and then make changes to it. This is, of course, a desirable and efficient way to proceed, since you can retain that which has not changed, you can limit updating to that which has changed since the last update, you can easily identify what has to be deleted as no longer applicable, and you generally can feel secure that you have not "missed anything." However, your competitors will be reviewing these documents the same way. Not only will they read the latest one, but they will (or at least should) read older editions to assemble a picture of what has changed.

You can try to make this more difficult, if not defeat it entirely, by restructuring the document once it is done, or, even better, having someone redo the document from scratch (without reference to the older one), a sort of "reengineering" process. There are several benefits of this approach. First, you make it more difficult for competitors to assemble a picture of your enterprise, in particular its changes. Second, you are also taking a fresh look at the entire document. By doing this, you are more likely to eliminate vestigial elements that have stayed in merely because they were not affirmatively deleted in the past. Third, you are more likely to add new items and information which are important, while omitting those items which are no longer relevant to your audience.

Directories and Surveys: Who Is Asking?

One of the fastest growing areas in commercial publishing is the directory or specialized reference handbook. Each year it seems there are more and more of these being published, either in hard copy, electronically, or both. But where do they get their information? Most companies assume they get the information from public sources, such as SEC filings, UCC reports, and the like. That is correct, as far as it goes, but many of these publishing firms use surveys, questionnaires, and telephone interviews to generate new data, to supplement information obtained from public sources, or to collect information. And they more and more often turn to you—the target—for that information.

Take, for example, the well-known Hoover series. The *Hoover's Handbook of American Business 1996* advertises that it now includes "indepth profiles of . . . major U.S. public and private companies, including operations overviews, company strategies, histories, up to 10 years of key financial data, lists of products, [and] executives' names."[21] To get that information, Hoover had to contact the firms, and the firms had to cooperate, at least to some degree. The same is true with respect to industry-specific directories.

For most firms, there is a benefit to being listed in these directories. That, in turn, means most companies will try to cooperate with publishers in their efforts to update these directories. While some firms may refer all such requests to a central person or group to handle, mainly to assure consistency and to minimize burdensomeness, rarely do those answering undertake an effort to make sure that the survey is legitimate. You should make sure that any such request is legitimate whether it is referred to one place.

Another growing area is the customer survey. Virtually all firms in most lines of business are urged to become "customer driven." This, in turn, usually generates an effort to understand existing customers, usually through a survey.[22] The result is that many firms are inundated with requests to answer questions about their relationships with key suppliers. While the vast majority of these inquiries are legitimate and proper, too many firms fail to assure themselves that the information is being collected for a supplier and not for a competitor.[23]

Feel Free to Limit Information Use by Others

There is no inalienable right for firms doing business with you to disclose that information. In the competitive intelligence business, for example, some consulting firms (including that of the authors) routinely enter into agreements protecting clients from having trade secrets or confidential information disclosed to third parties. However, most of our clients also take advantage of our willingness to permit them to bar disclosing the fact of their *retention* as well.

Consider that concept in other contexts. For example, one of the "Baby Bells" was the subject of a newspaper column dealing with its efforts to hire telephone operators. The Baby Bell was being put on the spot, since it had previously fired a number of operators. It was asked why it was hiring, after firing, operators. Even at the risk of losing some potentially valuable positive press, the reply was as follows: "The company spokesperson] said long-distance companies, whom she declined to identify because of their contractual arrangements with [the firm], are hiring [the firm] to provide directory assistance services."[24] The spokesperson protected information on its client.

Where Else Does Data Emerge?

For most firms, a Cloaking Program would seem to entail a careful review of all corporation filings with public agencies, particularly those with the U.S. SEC. However, it is not just *your* filings that are a window on your enterprise. Those with whom you do business may disclose more than you do. For example, in one annual report, Worthington Industries summarized its joint ventures. Among them was the Worthington Armstrong Venture (WAVE). WAVE was described as a joint venture with Armstrong World Industries and was characterized as "one of the largest producers of metal ceiling grid systems in the world," a quantifiable description.[25]

In its report filed for the same year, the other partner, Armstrong, did not discuss the size of WAVE. It did note that WAVE had opened a new plant in Nevada "to support growing grid sales in the Western U.S.," and that for the segment supported by the WAVE joint venture, "European sales [have] a significant impact."[26] The result was that Worthington provided details on the joint venture which it seems that Armstrong preferred were not made public.

Casual Conversations

Teach your employees to be careful about what they say and, perhaps more important, where they say it. Take, for example, elevators. Many large offices are spread over several floors in office buildings. In most firms, the employees use the elevators serving all floors (or even their bank of floors) to go from one to another.

Over time, employees become accustomed to seeing other people on the elevators. And with that comes comfort—and mistakes. All too often, employees will continue conversations in an elevator, even when they see someone in it already. A few, more cautious and already amenable to a cloaking mentality, will usually halt conversations when they see someone already in the car. But there are very few who will fully stop if the person they see looks familiar. For most of us, a familiar person is a person in the background. We tend to continue our conversation since we see no threat from the familiar. But talking in those circumstances is wrong. Familiar is not the same as safe. It is true that the familiar passenger may be someone else from another floor, working for the same firm you do, or he could be a contractor, working for your firm, servicing copiers. But have you ever considered that this service person could also be servicing copiers at a competitor's site, or married to someone working for a competitor?

Speaking in front of a stranger could be even more serious. That familiar face could belong to someone working for a competitor, coming back for interviews again and again. Has anyone considered what happens when he or she goes back to his or her employer, having failed to get a job? It could just be someone engaged to a coworker, but do you know where that person works? Where do his or her friends work? Think about it.

Consider adopting the policy illustrated by a sign in the elevator at St. Joseph's Hospital, Reading, Pennsylvania. There, each elevator, shared by patients, staff, and visitors, carries a notice to the effect that patient cases are not to be discussed in public places—which includes on elevators.

NOTES

1. On protecting trade secrets in litigation, see Chapter 10.
2. See, for example, "The Call for Full Disclosure," *CFO*, December 1994, 30–33, 36, 41–42.
3. Mellon Bank Corporation, *1994 Annual Report*, inside front cover.
4. Mellon Bank Corporation, *1995 Annual Report*.
5. Ibid., see particularly 6–16.
6. Mellon Bank Corporation, *1994 Annual Report*, inside front cover.
7. What is also not widely known is that U.S. corporations subject to our securities laws do not have to provide annual reports, 10-Ks, and so on to everyone. Technically, their obligation runs to shareholders and to filings with

the SEC, relevant exchange, and so on. In theory, at least, a public corporation could refuse to send its reports to competitors.

8. See, for example, Chapter 5.

9. These might be post office boxes for individuals, names without titles or affiliations, or cities where your competitors are located.

10. Kevin D. Murray, "Ten Spy-Busting Secrets," Internet home page publication, 1997, http://expertpages.com/news/spybust.htm.

11. Wire service report, "Judge Rules on E-Mail Privacy Case," 20 April 1997, posted on ar-news@environlink.org.

12. This term is credited to Joyce Graff. See Jenny C. McCune, "This Message is for You," *Beyond Computing*, June 1996, 39–41.

13. Ibid.

14. In a related arena, the use of the Internet for commerce also raises some interesting issues about information and privacy. See U.S. Congress, Congressional Budget Office, *Emerging Electronic Methods for Making Retail Payments* (Washington, D.C.: U.S. Government Printing Office, 1996), 35–48.

15. See Kelly Jackson Higgins, "Swarming Your Sites," *CommunicationsWeek*, 8 April 1996, 37. See also Anne Caluori, "Finding a Home on the Net," *Beyond Computing*, July/August 1996, 36; Anne Caluori, "Web Sales: Not Just Consumer Products," *InformationWeek*, 11 November 1996, 86–87.

16. "The Reality of Insecurity Hits Home," *InformationWeek*, 30 September 1996, 10.

17. This is quite separate from the issue of accidental (or purposeful) eavesdropping on cellular and mobile telephone conversations: "Some scanner users listen in on cellular phone calls. Others tap into their neighbors' cordless phone calls. . . . Says Harold Ort, editor of *Popular Communications* magazine, . . . 'But always assume someone is listening.'" "Someone is Listening," *U.S. News & World Report*, 27 January 1997, 14.

18. Murray, 1997.

19. "Cellular Privacy Tips," *Mobile Computing & Communications*, April 1997, 18.

20. Productivity, Inc., "Planning & Implementing TPM Workshop," (direct mail flyer) Dec. 1996–April 1997. However, nowhere on the form was a registrant asked in what industry it operates, making this promise somewhat hard to enforce.

21. The Reference Press, Inc., "Hoover's Handbooks," direct mail flyer, HH96.

22. See, for example, Keith L. Bond, "Survey Customers to Enhance Retention," *Rough Notes*, September 1996, 18–20, 89.

23. An unrelated problem, but a problem nonetheless, is a growing concern on how companies handle the "huge databases of customer-specific information, some of which is sensitive." See John Foley, "Data Dilemma," *InformationWeek*, 10 June 1996, 14–15; and H. Jefferson Smith, "How Private Are Personal Databases?" *Beyond Computing*, May 1996, 14–15. It would only become a cloaking issue if the firm allowed outsiders to have any access to it.

24. Mark Abrams, "Bell Atlantic Puts Out Call for Operators," *Reading [Pennsylvania] Eagle/Times*, 27 September 1996, B1.

25. Worthington Industries, Inc., *1996 Annual Report*, 3.

26. Armstrong World Industries, Inc., *Annual Report 1995*, 8, 24.

9

Cloaking Precepts: Where to Act

PRECEPT 7: IF YOU CANNOT PREVENT DISCLOSURE, CONCEAL SOME OF IT

Completely preventing competitively critical data from being accessible to your competitors is the ideal profile for a cloaked competitor. When that is not possible, you can still maintain your status as a cloaked competitor by the careful use of techniques designed to conceal (or mask) critical elements of that competitive sensitive data.

SEC Filings

One vital area to watch for unintended disclosure of competitively sensitive information deals with the numerous documents which are attachments to annual reports, quarterly reports, and the like filed with the U.S. SEC. Many companies forget (or were never even aware) that they are permitted to block out small amounts of critical information in these documents, even though the documents themselves must be made public.

While firms filing with the SEC cannot withhold critical information (such as markups and fees) from the SEC itself, they can keep it from being accessed by their competitors. To do this, a firm must first apply to the SEC under SEC Rule 24b-2 for permission. In that application, the firm must show, among other things, that the information it is seeking to protect from disclosure is the type regarded as confidential under the FOIA rules of the SEC. If permission is given by the SEC, then the firm marks the entire document as "CONFIDENTIAL TREATMENT." It also marks each specific approved deletion as "Confidential information omitted and filed separately with the Securities and Exchange Commission." While the data so protected will not be released to the public with the filing itself, that information will eventually have to be released. But it will be released years later, when confidential treatment is no longer needed for competitive reasons.

Seminar Attendance

Most firms send employees to seminars and conferences during the year. As a cloaking competitor, ask yourself what happens when your employees register for that meeting. Your employees dutifully provide their name, address, title, telephone number, and the like. The seminar producers will exercise care to make sure this information is kept confidential—from *their* competitors. They do that by marking these attendance lists as confidential. If they distribute the lists to attendees, they may provide only incomplete information, or seed the list with false names. The idea is to be able to keep competitors of the seminar producers from using these lists to generate attendees, as well as to be able to tell who is improperly using their list of attendees to promote their own seminar. However, very few of the seminar producers actually take steps aimed at protecting the identities of attendees and their employers.

Think about the last workshop you attended. Did your badge contain your name? What else did it contain? It might have included your title, your division, and your firm name. Why? Because that is the way we do it. To enhance a Cloaking Program, consider limiting the information you let the seminar producer put on your badge, by limiting what you give them in the registration materials or at sign-in. Try to have your badge and registration-list information limited to employee name and firm. Eliminate identifiers such as position title and subsidiary/SBU/project identification.[1] In fact, seriously consider having all employees identify themselves with the ultimate parent (or with a subsidiary with very low visibility) to minimize their own profile at the session.

As sensitivity to information disclosures increases, seminar producers may be expected to cooperate with and eventually assist firms in such efforts. A few producers may seek to go further—perhaps too far. Consider the following notice from a workshop on competitive intelligence. Does it make you feel more or less secure about attending? "What to ex-

pect: Anonymity: An alias seminar ID will be used to maintain confidences
and discourage distractions, including collection by third parties."[2]

Internet "Surfing"

Moving throughout the Internet, by surfing from site to site, is increasing exponentially. In part this is because the Internet is viewed as
a potential source for some of the raw data needed to develop CI.

It is gradually becoming well-known that Internet surfers do not do
so invisibly. In fact, current Internet site management systems can collect a significant amount of information on those accessing the site,
including the following:

- What city you are from.
- Last World Wide Web page visited.
- Your own e-mail address.
- Your favorite image at a site you visited.
- What kind of computer you are using.
- Your next Web destination.

As Web sites and their support technology improves, it is anticipated
that the amount of data they can, and will, collect on visitors will increase radically. The increase in data collected will permit advanced
profiling of Web users, with accompanying loss of personal and corporate privacy (and associated increases in advertising directed at surfers and their employers).[3]

There are at least two lessons to be learned from this. First, never
assume that your visit to any Web site is anonymous. If you are checking on a competitor's Web site, consider doing it from somewhere other
than your office's own net. Otherwise, repeated visits may tip off your
competitor about your interest. On the other hand, consider whether
your site is capable of alerting you to repeated visits from competitors.

Second, if you are conducting sensitive CI on the Internet, consider
using an intermediate site, called an anonymous remailer. These Internet
services strip away the header on your message so that recipients do not
know where it came from. From your perspective as a cloaked competitor, consider whether this extra effort is important to keep your competitors from finding out how many "hits" you have made on their site.

Foiling Data Mining and Mapping

Data-mining programs are designed to search numerous databases
and other computerized files to extract "hidden" relationships among
numerous factors. Their use today is chiefly, although not exclusively,

in the arena of customers and marketing decision making. The databases which they use are generally internal databases containing information on purchases and consumer profiles. However, the use of data mining and the application of this technology will shortly be expanded to searching through databases containing vast amounts of unprocessed raw data on competitors and related subjects.

According to one report, most data-mining programs are run using Occam's Razor (and a related principle) to sort and then highlight relationships. Occam's Razor is the principle which holds that explanations should be pared down to the simplest possible set of factors. The related principle used in data mining is called the Assumption of Similarity. That involves comparing a problem to known solutions.

A researcher in Australia took a popular data-mining program that was guided by both Occam's Razor and the Assumption of Similarity but gave precedence to Occam's Razor. The scientist, Dr. Webb, then changed the program to make the Assumption of Similarity the preferred approach. The primary difference between approaches is that using the Assumption of Similarity generates more complex results than using Occam's Razor. Dr. Webb then tested the program "for various decision-making tasks where the best outcomes were known. The decision trees' developed by the similarity assumption technique were significantly better."[4] The lesson is that different software data-mining approaches can produce different analyses using the same data. For the cloaked competitor, understanding the approach a competitor is using against you may help you to minimize the timely detection of competitively sensitive relationships.

There is a caveat. Do not underestimate how effective a data-mining program can and will be when applied to CI. As with so much else, the scope and speed of such programs is expanding rapidly. One expert has stated that while "humans are good with a small number of variables—no more than eight," there are databases which can operate "with hundreds or [even] thousands of variables."[5]

Mapping programs are a variant of data-mining programs. Mapping programs, currently used by criminal investigative agencies, are already capable of mapping and displaying complex, multilayered relationships, such as tracing how criminal groups support each other. As one mapping program vendor puts it, "Relationships that are hidden in text or numerical formats become obvious in a visual format, permitting rapid identification of analysis of relationships in large and seemingly unrelated data sets."[6]

Still, there are still two key limitations. First, the program must have the time to run its repeated sorting of records (up to days in some cases). Second, and more important, it must have a vast amount of raw data on which to operate. The best defense against both data mining and mapping may be the same as against other CI techniques—data concealment.[7]

PRECEPT 8: IF YOU CANNOT CONCEAL IT, MAKE IT HARDER OR MORE COSTLY TO ACQUIRE

While keeping competitively sensitive data from a competitor is an effective way to prevent a complete analysis from being conducted, not all such data can always be protected. If permanent protection is not available, consider a less effective but still useful technique. Make access more difficult.

The principle involved here is not unlike that on which home security systems, including everything from deadbolt locks to home alarm systems, are sold. No security system can prevent a determined thief from breaking in, but the presence of something additional, a strong lock for example, which will delay entry or make the time available when inside shorter than expected, will usually result in the thief moving to another, more vulnerable target. So it is with CI—making access to competitively sensitive information more costly or just delaying that access may serve to frustrate an analyst who is already operating under common constraints such as a limited amount of money and time. In such cases, the analyst may be expected to terminate research or to focus his or her efforts on another target where it is more likely that he or she will be able to collect data.

Internet Home Pages

Increasingly, firms are using their Internet home pages as a way for potential customers to locate the nearest company contact, such as sales office, broker, distributor, retail outlet, or dealer, from which they can make a purchase. For example, in the insurance industry there are firms that list every sales office, with information on each one, including the name of the key contact there, the office address, telephone, fax, and so on. The aim of the list is to make it easy for potential customers to find a nearby agent or broker so that they will make contact when they are ready to buy. However, this wealth of information also makes it easy for a competitor to generate a complete list of all of these offices, with virtually no effort.

A Cloaking Program should not try to keep this information from potential customers, as that would be counterproductive. However, the cloaked competitor should seek ways to make it more difficult for competitors to access all of it at once. That means the cloaking competitor must differentiate between the needs of the potential customer, who only wants to find one or two names of the closest offices or facilities, and the competitor, who wants a full profile list.

To accommodate your potential customers while frustrating your competitors, you might consider using the approach taken by one insurer. "The agency locator service on the . . . website makes agent addresses and telephone numbers available *based on city, state and ZIP code searches.*"[8] For the customer, this means that a nearby agent can be located by entering a state or ZIP code, and the home page will respond with a list of offices in that area. However, for a competitor to generate the full list of offices, the competitor must repeat the search fifty times, if the search can be done on a state-by-state basis. Already you have slowed down a competitor. If you wish to slow down competitors even more, you could eliminate state-level responses to requests. Instead, you would let the home page provide only city, ZIP code, or area code searches and then produce results listing offices strictly on a regional or county level. Then, the number of searches a competitor has to complete to generate a complete list increases explosively, while your potential customers still make one search.

Corporate and Subsidiary Names

> "They're always changing corporation names."
>
> Jefferson Starship,
> "We Built This City on Rock and Roll"

One of the ways in which CI researchers are frustrated in conducting research, particularly those using database searches, arises because of changes in corporate names. For example, if a corporation has changed its name over time, such as due to a merger, a search starting with the current name and going backward may well miss some references to predecessor businesses. But this problem is not limited to changes in a parent corporation's name. If a new unit was created within a company to carry on a particular project, and that new unit's name is rarely associated with the establishing parent, a search on either name alone will also probably miss many hits on the other name.[9] Finally, if an SBU has been sold by one firm to anther, a database search on the current parent, as opposed to on the unit itself, will quickly come to an inexplicable halt. A database searcher will find that, for no apparent reason, there are no citations before a particular year.

To the Cloaking Program, this means that identification of a product with a particular unit or subsidiary in press releases and the like may not always be desired. Such identifications may facilitate both future and historical research using databases.

Graphics and Printing

In the 1970s, as a reaction to the proliferation of high-quality copiers, office paper manufacturers began to produce "copy-proof papers." These papers were touted as being virtually impossible to duplicate on existing dry copiers. The goal was to allow firms to produce a document which could not be duplicated in minutes. The way this was accomplished varied, but generally was based on the fact that most copiers of that generation could not distinguish between some red and some black tones. Thus, for example, a pale red paper on which a contract was typed looked, to the copier, like black typing on a gray (or black) page. The resulting copy was just a gray-looking page. As copiers improved in quality, the ability of paper makers to foil them declined rapidly. With the advent of the color copier and then digital copying, the concept of "tricking" copiers fell into disuse.

Today, however, there are still ways to use graphics to at least slow down dissemination of some copied materials. For example, many fax machines and scanners still cannot easily separate printed matter from complex colored patterns serving as background to a display. All but the very top-of-the-line copiers produce confusing and unreadable copies of bar and pie charts when the charts use subtle shades of the same color to represent different items. Even when a copy of a document is not completely unintelligible, a second copy, fax, or scan of the first copy may be partially or even completely unreadable, particularly with respect to charts and graphs.

To the Cloaking Program, this means that you can sometimes foil efforts to copy or fax key segments of materials by the use of "busy" backgrounds, or through the use of shading or tints of the same color in displays. If you are not sure of how effective this can be, look at the color pictures in annual reports to shareholders filed with the SEC. Many of these color pictures are poorly reproduced by the commercial services copying filed annual reports to shareholders and then selling them to private companies.

The SEC's requirements for making electronic filings of required reports means that the pictures and graphics used in the glossy annual report to shareholders are not yet a part of the electronic files at the SEC, which are already accessible through the Internet. There are no indications whether or not the SEC will require the annual reports to shareholders to be filed in an electronic format, with all pictures, charts, and other illustrations electronically filed as well.

Freedom of Information Act

In the words of John Fialka, "FOIA was created by Congress in 1996, pushed by newspapers, magazine, and television editors intent on widening the public's view of government records. Since then, however, it has become a much bigger business, driven primarily by corporations seeing what government files can tell them about their competition."[10]

Assume that your competitors are seeking information on your current research-and-development capabilities. One option may be to identify any federal government contracts that have been awarded to your firm. Then, under the FOIA, the competitors can get copies of the contract which was awarded to you so they can study the specifications for the contract.[11] In addition, reports that you make to the agency which awarded that contract are often obtainable under the FOIA as well. You can immediately see how sensitive these data might be, as it could quickly reveal just how far your research and development has progressed, as indicated by the kinds of technology you use to perform under the contract.

What options do you have? You do not have a lot of flexibility, since the agency awarding the contract has its own rules to meet and reports to make. That does not mean, however, that you have no options. For example, in your response to the proposal you might want to note that you will ask that portions of your reports be kept in confidence under the provisions of the FOIA. Then, when the contract has been awarded, you should review your contract. If it is not barred by the contract, you can formally request that portions of your required reports be labeled as confidential and kept from disclosure under FOIA as they contain confidential information.

You should realize that marking these items as confidential does not guarantee that they will be kept from competitors. However, the FOIA requires that the agency notify you if it intends to release them at the written request of another party, so that you will at least have a opportunity to make your case to the agency that they be kept in confidence. Of course, that request may be denied. But it could take months for that request to be processed by the agency, thereby slowing your competitor's access to these items.[12]

Monitoring State and Local Legislation

As a part of being a cloaked competitor, your firm should be on the lookout for legislative or regulatory changes which may have unintended impacts on your Cloaking Program. For example, in 1996, California voters were presented with (and eventually rebuffed) a ballot initiative on securities law reform. This effort, called Proposition 211, was aimed at making it easier for shareholders to bring and prevail in suits against corporations under California's securities laws.[13]

While most attention was focused on its efforts to allow punitive damages in fraud cases and to expose directors to personal liability, Proposition 211 would have had other, cloaking-related impacts:

- It would have exposed corporations to suits for erroneous earnings projections.
- It would have allowed investors to sue companies when the company stock dropped because directors "willfully, knowingly or recklessly" made untrue statements about the company's prospects.

- It might have permitted suits alleging that directors failed to alert investors as to problems such as might arise in manufacturing or product launches.

As you can see, all these impacts would have limited the willingness and even the ability of firm's officers and directors to issue several classes of statements. By penalizing certain types and classes of statements, Proposition 211 would probably have caused most firms to refrain from making any statements which might trigger Proposition 211 lawsuits, thus cutting down on what all California firms put into the public domain.

You should also be sensitive to the collateral consequences of expanded requirements for filings with state governments. In some cases, the efforts may be more overt, aimed at forcing disclosure of information previously not disclosed or disclosable. Remember, in the long run almost all filings tend to become public, even if they are initially to be held in confidence.

Such disclosure efforts occurred in Massachusetts, where the state legislature became embroiled in efforts to force the tobacco industry to "divulge the exact ingredients . . . in each brand of cigarettes, cigars, and chewing tobacco." Lobbyists for the tobacco industry argued that the law, which was aimed at giving consumers more information on what they are smoking in order to get them to stop, would force them to reveal "trade secrets."[14] It is probable that, if such a law passed, it would eventually be expended to cover other consumer products.

Legislative changes that impact your Cloaking Program do not have to be at the state or federal level to have a significant effect on your business. For example, the way in which local governments enforce open-records laws can either provide a powerful defense against those seeking to access your filings, or, conversely, can make it (from your point of view) too easy to gain such access. Take, for example, efforts by a Pennsylvania municipality to deal with a large number of requests to see public records dealing with a particular controversy. That municipality required anyone interested in seeing any public documents to (1) make an appointment, (2) provide a written request for the records, and (3) pay 25 cents per page requested, with a minimum charge of $5.[15]

Such policies would have made access to the disputed documents, as well as all other documents filed in that township, more cumbersome. That, in turn, might discourage CI data-collection efforts targeting locally filed data where those data are seen as probably having minimal value when balanced against the cost and inconvenience of getting them.

Surveys

There may be times when your firm wishes to provide input for a survey. In particular, there has been an increase in surveys which are generated by private research firms who, in turn, sell the results to companies in the market segments being surveyed. In some cases the surveys are actually sponsored by firms in the industry, possibly including yours. Such sponsorship carries with it some advantages, as the participating firms get the resulting report some months, or even a year, before the general public does, and the participating firms get the report at a significantly lower price than that charged to nonparticipating firms.

You should make inquiries before replying to such a survey, or before agreeing to underwrite it. Ask who will eventually be able to access the entire survey results, regardless of when that access occurs. In other words, if you cannot keep the report from becoming public, you can limit sales of it only to those who contribute to it so the price of obtaining access to data on your firm is providing data on their own firm.

PRECEPT 9: THE TOP MAY BE HARDER TO CONTROL THAN THE BOTTOM

One often-overlooked problem in establishing a Cloaking Program is that the very most senior executives in a firm are often the most resistant to cooperating, or at least are the most likely to let slip competitively sensitive nuggets. This is probably because of the fact that these executives work every day with vast amounts of data which meet that description and become desensitized to the impact of even side comments. These executives should be made aware of the fact that their speeches in any public forum, as well as any other remarks which they make in *any* context, will be the subject of intense scrutiny by their competitors.

Speaking Out

As we move into the Information Age, there are many groups seeking to have corporations "speak out" on many issues, and there are corporations which are responding to such pressures. For example, in October 1996, the Chairman of USX Corporation urged business leaders to "stand up for the moral values they believe in."[16] As a part of that same speech, he also urged businesses to "communicate with all of our stakeholders." The aim of that communication was to have businesses let stockholders, employees, customers, and the local community know what was going on with a company. Such communication is fraught with risks to a Cloaking Program, in that it is communications to stockholders, employees, customers, and the local community which are most often targeted by CI professionals for important raw data.

Corporations do not seem to be particularly sensitive to this. For example, "[USX Chairman] Usher said he has never been told by any employee that the company was giving them too much information." We feel sure that he definitely was never told that by a competitor either.

How Secret Is Secret?

In mid-1997, McDonald's Corporation found itself locked in a "war" with its fast-food competitors. That conflict saw all parties seeking to develop and exploit advantages by changes in product offerings, pricing, and promotional support. However, depending on which officer was speaking, McDonald's seemed to operating under conflicting concepts of how "secret" its marketing plans were. Compare these two contemporaneous reports in the media. First, "McDonald's last month knocked the price of breakfast sandwiches and then Big Macs down to 55 cents. . . . Each month is set to highlight a different sandwich; June's will be the Quarter Pounder with Cheese, and July's [targeted sandwich] is still a closely guarded secret,"[17] and second, "[McDonald's] President Ed Rensi said the company would be stepping up local ads and market-specific initiatives to reinforce 'Campaign 55', which is being extended today to the Quarter Pounder with Cheese for 55 cents with purchase of fries and a drink. . . . Also, [McDonald's] chairman Michael Quinlan expressed enthusiasm for what he termed, 'Some real hot new chicken stuff that might be coming out before you know it.'"[18]

NOTES

1. For examples of what tactics may be used at meetings, see Chapter 8.

2. LKM Research, *Food for Thought: You Are What You Eat* (direct mail announcement), July–September, 1996.

3. See, for example, "Mission Anonymous," *U.S. News & World Report*, 17 June 1996, 76; "How to Practice Safe Surfing," *Business Week*, 9 September 1996, 120–121.

4. "So Much for the Principle of Similarity," *Business Week*, 2 September 1996, 81.

5. Usama Fayyad, quoted in "Coaxing Meaning Out of Raw Data," *Business Week*, 3 February 1997, 134, 137.

6. The NETMAP® Software System from Alta Analytics, Dublin, Ohio, 1996.

7. Curiously, a completely opposite approach, overloading a competitor with information, may work, at least in the short run. "Data overload can quickly paralyze a [data mining-based] decision-making process." See Jenny C. McCune, "Checking Out the Competition," *Beyond Computing*, March 1996, 24, 29; "Too many hits are just as useless as no hits at all." James Derk, "Net Sites for Journalists," *Online User*, July/August 1996, 20.

8. "Agency Website is a 'hit,'" *The [Nationwide] Challenger*, July 1996, 1. Emphasis added.

9. For example, Saturn, which is a unit of GM.

10. John J. Fialka, *War by Other Means: Economic Espionage in America* (New York: W. W. Norton, 1997), 130.

11. The winning bid is usually also available (while the losing ones are not). However, most agencies warn bidders to clearly label all confidential information to keep it from being disclosed under FOIA.

12. Note that the request must be made when you file. The position of federal agencies seems to be that a request to protect data made after filing the documents containing the data "has no influence on the releasing of FOIA information." U.S. Forest Service spokesperson, quoted in "Government Accused of Hiding Logging Plans," Associated Press, in *Reading [Pennsylvania] Eagle/Times*, 12 May 1997, A12.

13. See, for example, Julie Schmidt, "Learch: Silicon Valley's Nightmare," *USA Today*, 23 October 1996, B1–B2; Testa, Hurwitz, & Thibeault, "Memorandum to Clients: California Securities Law Ballot Initiative (Proposition 211) Defeated," 11/6/96, http://www.tht.com/ClientBulletinProp211.htm.

14. "Law would Demand Listing All Ingredients in Cigarettes," Associated Press, in *Reading* [Pennsylvania] *Eagle/Times*, 26 July 1996, A5.

15. See "Editorial: Fee for Records should Be Illegal," *Reading* [Pennsylvania] *Eagle/Times*, 26 September 1996, B8. That editorial noted that AT&T was engaged in a marketing campaign to convince local governments to use 900 numbers for calls for certain types of public record information.

16. Don Spatz, "Usher Says Firms Need to Voice Moral Issues," *Reading* [Pennsylvania] *Eagle/Times*, 9 October 1996.

17. "You Deserve a Translation Today," *U.S. News & World Report*, 2 June 1997, 54.

18. "McDonald's Testing Service, Product-Quality Enhancements," *Nations' Restaurant News Online*, 23 May 1997, http://www.nrn.com.

10

Your Cloaking Program: Organizational Issues

Traditionally, businesses have viewed the "defensive" world of competitive intelligence as separate and apart from the "offensive" activities of CI. Thus, defending corporate information as an asset has typically encompassed efforts such as the appropriate use of intellectual-property protections and corporate security programs.[1] The legal underpinning of intellectual-property protection includes patents and trademarks, trade-secrets laws, as well as legal instruments, such as nondisclosure contracts.

We have chosen to call what we advocate a Cloaking Program to distinguish it from these activities and protections. A Cloaking Program is just that—a program. It is not a project to be undertaken by one unit as its sole responsibility. Rather, as with competitive intelligence itself, it is more of a process, impacting and being impacted by related processes.[2] But, as you will soon understand, operating a Cloaking Program requires understanding and even coordinating with some, if not all, of these efforts.

CLOAKING PROGRAMS AND CLASSIC CORPORATE
INFORMATION DEFENSE ACTIVITIES

Intellectual-Property Protection Programs[3]

Classic intellectual-property programs involve the careful use of the varied legal protections provided by patents, trademarks, copyrights, and associated laws. While the legal protection provided by these laws can be formidable, these legal regimes all have one requirement in common: The materials, ideas, concepts, invention, designs, and so on being protected must all necessarily be disclosed to the public, including to your competitors, in order to become protected by law.

In the area of patent law, protection is provided based on filings with the U.S. government. The degree of protection is predicated on what is filed. To put it in an overly simplistic manner, if you do not file it (where it can be reviewed by the public), you cannot protect it. And patent protection terminates after a period of time.

In the areas of trademarks, service marks, copyrights, and the like, your firm must claim a right to use the protected works, designs, or the like. This is accomplished both by using them and by marking them with distinctive marks, such as ™, ©, ®, or the equivalent in words. These two actions establish your claims to legal protection. In addition, there are filing requirements to be met for additional protection.

Thus, you can see that the use of these protections is actually antithetical to a Cloaking Program, in that they mandate disclosure to secure protection. In fact, as discussed in Chapter 5, CI has developed a number of analytical processes which are actually keyed to the fact that patents, in particular, are public and that the inventor must provide significant amounts of important information in support of the application. These techniques allow careful and skilled CI professionals to develop some very interesting intelligence assessments, based almost exclusively on the filed public materials.

Trade Secret Laws

There are two basic legal schemes which now impact the collection of any intelligence: the Uniform Trade Secrets Act and the Economic Espionage Act of 1996. They impact the collection of intelligence because they limit what those collecting economic and competitive information can do vis-à-vis trade secrets. It is critical to know about these laws because they apply to everyone in the U.S. marketplace and affect the way that they operate with respect to trade secrets. If your competitor violates them, it may face civil or even criminal liability. However, to trigger those legal protections, you must be very careful in the ways that you handle and protect your trade secrets. To acquaint you with these laws, we will *quickly* take you through them together. First, you should appreciate that we are dealing with statutes aimed at trade secrets only. Second, there is law covering this area at both the federal and state level.

At the state level there are two types of civil protections for trade secrets. Forty states have already enacted laws which are all variations of the UTSA, last revised in 1985. In the remaining states, their common law (or judge-made law) also protects trade secrets.[4] State common law generally utilizes the same principles as set forth in the UTSA.[5] An additional level of protection is now provided by the new federal criminal law, the EEA.[6]

State Laws. Under state laws, a business can bring a civil suit for damages that were caused by misappropriation of a trade secret. Under UTSA, and similarly under the common law of states that have not adopted the UTSA, each of these concepts is a carefully defined term.

Under the UTSA, a trade secret is information of virtually any sort, including a formula, pattern compilation, program, device, method, or process that (1) derives economic value from not "being generally known to, and not being readily ascertainable by proper means by" other people or companies who could gain economic value from getting and using it, and (2) is subject to "efforts that are reasonable under the circumstances to maintain its secrecy."

Misappropriation of a trade secret requires the existence of one of two critical steps: Either (1) somewhere along the line the trade secret is acquired by anyone who knows or should know that the trade secret was acquired by improper means, or (2) the person who gets the trade secret knows or should know that it was a trade secret and that it has been acquired by accident or mistake. That means, in short, a claim of misappropriation under state law arises only when both of two key events have happened. First, someone obtains, uses, or discloses another person's trade secret, and second, the person against whom the claim of misappropriation is made (1) acquired the trade secret by improper means, (2) knew or should have known that somewhere along the line the trade secret was acquired by improper means, (3) knew or should have known that the trade secret was acquired by accident or mistake, or (4) knew or should have known that somewhere along the line the trade secret was disclosed in violation of a confidentiality provision.

If there is a violation of the UTSA, then the company that is injured has a variety of options open to it through legal actions which it can bring in state court. It can seek an injunction to stop an actual or even a threatened misappropriation of a trade secret. In some cases the injunction may even allow the company to collect royalties as damages.

An injured company can also seek a court order to compel someone to affirmatively protect a trade secret which has come into his or her hands. The company can recover damages for misappropriation. Those damages cover both any actual loss caused by the misappropriation as well as damages for the unjust enrichment caused by the misappropriation. An injured company may also be able to collect exemplary damages and attorney fees.

Federal Law. The EEA is in some ways very similar to the UTSA.[7] However, the key things to remember are that the EEA is a criminal law and it operates at the federal law. That means it applies in every state, whether or not the state has already adopted the UTSA. It also means that violators face jail sentences and fines. Under the EEA, a trade secret is virtually any type of information, in any form, where (1) the owner has taken "reasonable measures to keep such information secret," and (2) the information derives independent economic value "from not being generally known to, and not being readily ascertainable through proper means by, the public." This federal criminal law then penalizes theft and unauthorized duplication of a trade secret, as well as receipt and transfer of a trade secret.

Misappropriation of Trade Secrets. While this all seems comprehensive, there are several important concepts embodied in both the UTSA and the EEA which actually mean that their impact on *legitimate* competitive intelligence collection activities aimed at you is quite limited.

First, the information you are trying to protect with the UTSA and EEA must be able to be specifically identified. It is not enough to say that "everything here is a trade secret." To protect information, you must first identify it. Second, the information involved really must be a trade secret. One key to determining if this is the case is to ask the following question: Has what you are seeking to protect been the subject of reasonable efforts to keep it secret? If the answer is no, it cannot be a trade secret. For example, if it is a document and is stamped "Confidential" at the bottom of each page, you are well on the way to protecting it under the UTSA and the EEA. On the other hand, if the same document is included in promotional materials being given to thousands of customers, it is not a trade secret. Third, under both the EEA and UTSA, is the information you think you are protecting as a trade secret "readily ascertainable by proper means?" That statutory language in both laws means that the *deduction or reconstruction by proper means of what may in fact be a trade secret is not a violation of either law.* Deduction or reconstruction are not the same as misappropriation. And misappropriation is what is needed to trigger legal protections.

All this means that trade secret protection can be lost through disclosures, whether accidental or purposeful, made in any of the following common contexts:[8]

- Information is revealed in published literature, such as trade journal articles.
- Scholarly articles are published by in-house scientists containing information sought to be protected.

- Key data are disseminated in the form of technical bulletins to customers.
- A technical paper is delivered to a trade and professional group containing confidential information.
- Publication of "secret" matter is made in the background of photographs in an annual report.
- Performance data are partially revealed in an advertisement.
- Disclosures of company secrets are made by the company through course instructions to customers.
- Labels on products disclose "secret" ingredients and relative quantities of ingredients.
- Advertisements in newspapers and trade papers contain significant, previously undisclosed details.
- Important technical disclosures are made in operating instructions provided to customers.
- "Secret" products are displayed at a trade show.

Remember that *when your competitors obtain small pieces of intelligence, each of which has been found properly, and then their analysts eventually build a picture of your critical intentions, including a trade secret, which you have sought to keep secret, they have* not *broken any law.* They have just engaged in good solid CI collection and analysis.

For example, the Japan External Trade Organization is regarded by federal intelligence agencies as "the most sophisticated commercial-intelligence-gathering body operated by a foreign government on U.S. soil." However, "JETRO . . . is almost certainly complying with American law."[9] Given these limitations of statutory trade-secret protection, you must look to other options, including initiating a Cloaking Program, for broader assistance.

Legal Protection of Confidential Information

Confidential materials and information are not the same as trade secrets. While all trade secrets are kept in confidence, not all confidential materials are trade secrets. Confidential is a much wider concept. If a document is marketed as "confidential," an employee is expected to handle it carefully and to respect that marking. However, when an employee does not know that information is confidential, and that employee has not been told that it is confidential, the employee may not be obliged to keep it a secret. Because of this, employment, consulting, and independent contract agreements often provide that those signing the agreement agree not to reveal or to use any of the business's trade secrets or confidential information.

Contract restrictions dealing with confidential information are growing in popularity for several reasons. More businesses are sensitive to the importance of protecting themselves against the leak of confidential information to competitors, and these agreements have historically been relatively easy to enforce. For these two reasons, classic legal protections for sensitive corporate information have usually been found in the areas of nondisclosure agreements. The goal of the agreements is to create a legal obligation on the part of the employee, even after the employee leaves the employer, to protect the employer's competitive position by protecting certain classes of confidential information from disclosure to competitors.

In this way, if a third party, such as a competitor, obtains competitively sensitive data by inducing someone to violate a confidentiality obligation, that third party risks a lawsuit for inducing a breach of that obligation. That possibility exists whether the obligation of confidentiality is memorialized in a contract or derived from a common-law obligation that the person making the disclosure had to the owner of the confidential information.

However, such agreements do not provide perfect protection. For example, there is a critical distinction between the following two situations. The first involves inducing (or even forcing) someone to breach a confidentiality obligation to you, the scope of which your competitor knows will be breached by the disclosure of the information it seeks. The second is when your competitor asks your former employee for information that your competitor knows the employee has. However, the competitor does not know whether a written confidentiality obligation is in place, or even if there is an agreement, whether or not that agreement covers the information it is seeking. The first situation raises the legal issues described. The second situation may actually be legally and even ethically fine, but *only* as long as the competitor did not have any reason to know that the information was subject to a confidentiality obligation.

There are additional problems with these contract clauses. For example, what is confidential or a trade secret is a very important issue in using these clauses. Courts have ruled that a company cannot sue former employees to stop them from using trade secrets if these were not actually treated as trade secrets by the company seeking to enforce the clause. By analogy, if a company has not treated information as confidential, then it would be precluded from suing an employee for failing to respect an agreement to keep that same information confidential. Some companies have tried to get around this by asking employees to sign an agreement to bar the "use of any and all information gained" during employment or while a person is under contract. Such broad clauses are usually seen by the courts as unreasonable. For that reason, the courts will not enforce them, because to do so could forbid the disclosure of information that is actually common knowledge.

Legal, particularly contractual, controls over confidential information are limited in what they can protect against. While seeking to prevent release (by having an employee agree to protect the information), they do have an active aspect—their value ultimately lies in their ability to prevent the disclosure thorough legal action, or to collect financial damages for the violation of these agreements.

A highly controversial case, *Food Lion v. ABC News,* may serve as an example of the ways in which various legal tools can be applied to protect a business. As many in business may recall, ABC sent two reporters to apply for jobs with the retail food chain, Food Lion. When hired, they took undercover tapes (with hidden cameras) of what ABC felt was the sale of spoiled food. ABC then ran a television story on this, using some but not all of the tapes. Food Lion felt that its operations had been grossly misrepresented and took legal action. Food Lion eventually sued ABC for a variety of reasons and won, at the trial level, on several unusual grounds. Among them, the trial court found that ABC had committed fraud, trespass, and breach of loyalty.

Nowhere in this case was the issue of trade secrets raised. Yet Food Lion convinced the jury to award punitive damages against ABC based on how it operated, and not on what it showed.[10] What is of interest here is that Food Lion responded to an effort to learn about its corporate management policies by taking legal action based on a variety of legal protections.

Corporate Security Programs

Corporate security programs are traditionally aimed at the protection of corporate assets from assaults. That mission is often focused on physical and related security issues, as in preventing theft, breaking and entering, and the like. In recent years, the scope of responsibility has been expanded to protecting the company's intangible assets, such as software and computer records, from theft or damage (i.e., from hackers).

While a Cloaking Program certainly should raise the awareness of all employees to the competitive risks associated with such assaults on the firm, a Cloaking Program's scope of operations should be significantly broader. That is, the focus should be on protecting critical pieces of competitively sensitive information. The risk of theft or damage is only one small element of the overall risk.

However, an active corporate security program can help in the effort to create and operate a Cloaking Program. For example, while corporate security should properly be concerned about preventing improper access to corporate facilities, it can play other roles in support of the Cloaking Program. Specifically, corporate security could monitor the perimeters of corporate facilities for frequent "drive-bys," which might indicate a corporate intelligence initiative by a competitor. Corporate security could also review sign-in records to see if there are persons who may represent CI firms (a list of which could be obtained from the CI unit) but are there for unspecified reasons, and assist by training employees is security-oriented techniques, such as safe fax (see Chapter 8).

COMPETITIVE INTELLIGENCE UNITS IN CLOAKING COMPETITORS

Because the most frequent uses for a CI unit deal with focusing on your competitors and not on your own firm, one unit that you may not immediately consider keeping in the loop with respect to initiating the effort to create a Cloaking Program is your own competitive intelligence unit. That is because your own CI unit has the capability of undertaking defensive activities, as well as its already active offensive activities.

The difference between the offensive and the defensive use of CI is subtle, yet it may be critical. For example, using CI offensively can involve tracking the activities of current direct competitors on a regular basis. Offensive use could also involve developing profiles of their ongoing activities overall as well as prospective activities in a specific market niche of particular importance to you. If your firm is already a participant in that market niche, you would be checking on your relative position as a part of this effort, even though the CI effort is not aimed at your own firm.

In contrast, defensive CI activities involve monitoring and evaluating your own business's activities as your competitors and others perceive them. The difference from offensive CI is critical. Defensive CI is not an evaluation of what your firm can do or is doing. Rather, it involves developing data on how others, principally your competitors, see your business, even if their perception of your business is erroneous. Because it is not as focused as more traditional offensive CI, defensive CI usually entails the collection of larger amounts of less-focused data than is usually the case with offensive CI. However, it still requires following the same steps as are involved in developing CI.

For many firms, the most efficient way to combine the best of what your own unit can do with the objectivity of an outsider would be to have an outside firm provide regular (e.g., quarterly) reports on your firm as your competitors might see it. This task would be limited to one or two key areas each time. Your own CI unit would have the responsibility of maintaining regular monitoring activities between quarterly reports. The quarterly reports would also help the internal efforts by confirming their validity or correcting small perception errors before they become significant problems.

Defensive CI and Corporate Security Programs

Defensive CI is not the same as, and should not be confused with, corporate security programs. As noted, the scope of corporate security will range from efforts to reduce petty theft by employees to retaining a security firm to find the source of confidential computer records which are being leaked to competitors. None of those are within the scope of defensive CI. Rather, defensive CI is more properly considered as an internal countermeasure, even if it does involve protecting, or defending, against competitors obtaining data on you.

Case Studies

The following three case studies may help to illustrate the scope and utility of defensive CI.

In the first, a regional bank holding company (BHC) hired a well-regarded consultant to help it evaluate its strategic long-term options as they related to expansion and acquisitions. The retention made it clear to the consultant that one option to BHC was to enter into an aggressive acquisition program, another was to seek to be acquired, and a third was to erect defenses against any potential hostile takeover. This consultant, unknown to BHC, publicized its retention and the general nature of its assignment in the trade press. BHC quickly became viewed as a potential takeover candidate because of the retention of the consultant—the announcement of its hiring to the banking industry had actually "put it in play." In a brief period following the announcement, BHC received numerous propositions offering to acquire it. Because of this unanticipated focus, BHC was thus forced to decide more quickly than it anticipated whether to accept one of these overtures—solely because of the announcement.

The second case involved a major natural resources corporation (Resources) which acquired U.S. rights to an important new process developed in Europe. Before Resources had even acquired a trade name for the process, stories on the new process appeared in a major national news magazine and in both network and cable television reports. Resources felt compelled to make a public announcement about the process—well before the product which it would produce could even come on the market. Resource's understandable reluctance to make an announcement probably stemmed from the expected loss of future advertising impact. It now had to announce the process without being able to coordinate that announcement with a well-prepared marketing campaign.

In the third case, a Fortune 500 U.S. industrial corporation (Industry) found out that it had earlier been profiled as a prime potential takeover candidate by a Wall Street investment firm, in part because it was reluctant to sell off several of its operating divisions. Industry only became aware of this investment analysis report after it had been published in a business newspaper. By the time Industry read about the critical analysis, substantial blocks of Industry's stock had already been acquired by speculators who had had access to the underlying report and appeared to be acquiring the stock because of the report. Industry feared that they were acquiring and holding stock to sell to an acquiring company. Industry was quickly forced into a rapid and relatively unplanned restructuring. It began to sell off some operating divisions to prevent the completion of what threatened to become a self-fulfilling prophecy—its takeover by outsiders.

In each case, defensive CI—that is, checking on what your competitors knew about you—could well have prevented the businesses from being surprised. In fact, an effective defensive CI program could have minimized, if not eliminated, the consequences of these surprises.

In the first case, regular monitoring of regional business papers as well as of industry trade publications would have turned up the unexpected announcement as soon as it appeared. At that point, BHC could have responded and possibly prevented the inadvertent and unsought courtships.

In the second case, monitoring all announcements made by the European firm after the licensing agreement was signed might have disclosed that the European firm was making unexpected announcements about its new U.S. licensee. Knowing that, Resources could have avoided its virtually unplanned early announcement by contacting the European firm and asking it to curtail its announcements, or at least give Resources slightly more time to prepare for the now inevitable moment when it would have to respond to media reports.

In the third case, monitoring the reports and recommendations of investment bankers who tracked Industrial would have disclosed the takeover "warning" sooner and possibly avoided the self-fulfilling prophecy.

As these examples show, defensive CI can pay dividends. Some firms are unwilling, however, to devote the same levels of skill and amounts of work toward defensive CI as they routinely devote to the more traditional offensive CI. This is a mistake. Your competitors may already be devoting substantial resources and high levels of skill toward developing CI on your firm.

To be safe, in conducting defensive CI you should always credit your potential adversaries with being at least as efficient as you are in gathering CI. Thus, you should use your own CI skills and resources to monitor information about your own business just as you monitor that of your competitors. That means going to the same external sources and checking the same on-line databases, with the same regularity as you apply to your offensive CI work. It also means using the same analytical techniques, even if that produces information surprising to, or even unwanted by, senior management.

Defensive CI and Cloaking Programs

For the Cloaking Program, defensive CI provides yet another way to help identify where competitively sensitive information on your firm is available to your competitors, and what conclusions they can draw (and may already be drawing) about your actions. While defensive CI would permit you to minimize problems, such as those illustrated, a Cloaking Program might have helped avoid them.

Table 10.1 summarizes some key similarities and differences among the programs we have just discussed.

Table 10.1
Program Comparisons

Function	Cloaking Program	Corporate Security	Defensive Intelligence	Trade Secret Protection
Information/ Communication Coverage	Competitively Sensitive, or Leading to Same	Corporate Assets, includes Trade Secrets	Competitively Sensitive	Trade Secrets Only
Aimed at Preventing Damaging Disclosures	Yes	No, Aimed at Penetrations	No, Monitoring Them	Yes
Legal Support, Civil	No	Yes, Nondisclosure Agreements	No	Yes
Legal Support, Criminal	No	Yes, Actions for Theft, Trespass	No	Yes (Federal)
Contracts Involved	Yes	Yes	No	Yes
Defensive/Offensive	Both	Defensive	Defensive	Both

NOTES

1. One author has extended the warfare metaphor by offering up an analysis of "information warfare," involving "1. the distribution and dissemination of the disinformation and misinformation, 2. the destruction or modification of some key information, 3. unauthorized uses or theft of the valuable data and information and 4. the penetration of competitors' or other opponents' information systems and databases." Mark Saarelainen, *Information Warfare and Its Impacts on Commercial Enterprises*, December 1996 (Internet distribution, available from mjsus@ix.netcom.com).

2. See John J. McGonagle and Carolyn M. Vella, *A New Archetype for Competitive Intelligence* (Westport, Conn.: Quorum Books, 1996).

3. The scope of intellectual-property law is beyond the scope of this chapter, and even of this book. See the bibliography for additional references.

4. Some of these states may eventually adopt the UTSA as well.

5. Appendix B sets forth the full text of the UTSA. In addition, because of the importance of understanding what it does (and does not) impact with respect to CI, we have also republished the official comments of the experts who drafted this model law.

6. The full text of the EEA is also set forth in Appendix B. In spite of the fact that it was the subject of hearings for several years, the legislative history of what the law is intended to do is remarkably slender. To aid our readers, we have reprinted the only official section-by-section analysis of the almost-final version of the act, together with the few comments in the U.S. Senate and House of Representatives debate which bear on the act.

7. What is highly significant is that "The definition of the term 'trade secret' [in EEA] is based largely on the definition of that term in the Uniform Trade Secrets Act." *Economic Espionage Act of 1996*, 104th Cong., 2d sess., H. R. 104-788, 16 September 1996, 16. Thus, those seeking to understand the EEA should be guided by the UTSA (and its official comments).

8. Kenneth B. Weckstein and Sandra J. Boyd, "How to Obtain Competitors' Intelligence Legally . . . and How to Protect Your Own," in *Global Perspectives on Competitive Intelligence*, ed. John E. Prescott and Patrick T., Gibbons (Alexandria, Va.: Society of Competitive Intelligence Professionals, 1993), 281, 288.

9. "With Friends Like These," *U.S. News & World Report*, 16 June 1997, 46–48.

10. "ABC Ordered to Pay Chain $5.5 Million," Associated Press, in *Reading [Pennsylvania] Eagle/Times*, 23 January 1997, A3.

11

Using Your New Low Visibility

Now that you are convinced of the benefits of using cloaking and understand how to manage your competitively sensitive information to achieve the status of a cloaking competitor, there is more. It is time to begin to harvest the benefits of having an effective Cloaking Program. Remember, the goal here is not merely to be invisible (or partially visible) to your competitors. *It is to achieve that position and then use that low profile to achieve a competitive advantage.* As Sun Tzu put it in the military context hundreds of years ago, "By altering his arrangements and changing his plans, the skillful general keeps the enemy without definite knowledge. By shifting his camp and taking circuitous routes, he prevents the enemy from anticipating his purpose."[1]

Take a look at two last cases which help to show how operating with an effective Cloaking Program might help exploit your new competitive advantage.

CASE STUDIES

Typically, when a company introduces a new product or service, or is ready to do so, it takes particular care to make sure potential consumers know a great deal about the forthcoming product or service.

The reasoning is that the announcement is, at least in part, itself an element of the marketing of the product or service. That is, potential customers will have their interest piqued by trade reports, thus generating high recognition levels when the actual launch reaches them. That, in turn, means that when the announcement deals with a forthcoming product or service, the marketing strategy is usually to have the announcement describe all of the features, benefits, and so on of the new launch. The underlying belief is that potential consumers will not only begin to think how that product or service can be used by them, but, in some cases, may be "frozen." That is, the potential customers might hold off buying a competitor's arguably inferior current offering and wait for your offering to become available.

However, by adopting this strategy you surrender the element of surprise—you are not operating as a cloaked competitor. And you must always keep in mind that surprise can also work for you.

In fact, contrary to accepted belief, announcements of forthcoming new offerings to customers often engender skepticism, rather than generating high levels of anticipation. Take, for example, computer software, where the scope of promised software, when compared with the capability of the products actually eventually provided, is often deficient. In fact, many such offerings do not arrive on the marketplace when promised.[2]

Operating in such skeptical markets, a cloaked competitor may be able to create and maintain the image of a responsible and careful provider of goods and services. Take, for example, the clear surprise evidenced in an article in one trade magazine: "Corel Corp. is much further along in its development of a Java-based version of WordPerfect than the company let on when it announced its Java plans earlier this year."[3] Corel, operating as a cloaked competitor might act, had obviously withheld details of a new offering. The result is surprise—with just a touch of admiration for having not overpromised.

To close this book, we are returning to the subject of our very first case study, the Campbell Soup Company. As we noted in Chapter 3, in dealing with a story about its restructuring, Campbell Soup Company's behavior was consistent with a cloaking strategy. Some ten months later, *Business Week* reported on yet another change at that firm.[4] Campbell was in the midst of a new product launch for its "Intelligent Quisine" line. This line was a part of a program of dietetically correct foods, prepackaged and delivered weekly to consumers' homes.

What is implicit in the piece is that the information on the existence and scope of this program became available only when Campbell Soup wanted it to. In an industry as competitive as retail foods, it is a certainty that Campbell Soup Company was regularly monitored by its multinational competitors, such as Heinz, Nestlé, and ConAgra. Yet it managed to protect knowledge about the very existence of a new type of product line from reaching its competitors until its actual release.

The advantage? If Campbell Soup is correct in seeing this as a new market niche, it will have occupied it until its competitors, beginning from a cold start, can gear up. That much of a jump may be overwhelming—as ConAgra's successful (and surprising) launch of "Healthy Choice" years before illustrates, even to this day.

NOTES

1. Sun Tzu, *The Art of War*, ed. James Clavell (New York: Dell, 1983), 65–66.

2. These failures have caused observers to coin the term "vaporware," for software which exists only in concept.

3. "The Perfect Word: Java," *InformationWeek*, 2 September 1996, 24.

4. "Now, Campbell's Makes House Calls," *Business Week*, 16 June 1997, 144–145.

APPENDIXES

A

Disinformation

In contrast to the protective screening of a Cloaking Program, disinformation is a form of deception. Disinformation may be defined as incomplete or inaccurate information designed to mislead others about your intentions or abilities. When used in the arena of international politics, espionage, or intelligence, the term actually encompasses the deliberate production and dissemination of falsehoods, fabrications, and forgeries aimed at misleading an opponent or those supporting an opponent.

As the text of a secret U.S. government document on disinformation is reported to have said, disinformation "combines real and illusory events . . . with the basic goal of making (the target) *think* what the initiator wanted." According to this document, among the objectives of a disinformation plan is to keep the target "preoccupied" and "off balance."[1]

Disinformation is not the same as "puffing," a generally accepted form of advertising overstatement that falls short of fraud. For an example of such advertising overstatement, we can look at the 1997 pricing of automobiles for U.S. car makers:

In Detroit it's the year of the stealth price increase. . . . Chrysler Corp. triple-dipped on its star minivan, hiking its price in January, March, and July. It also slipped in an unannounced increase of $72 to $5000 on its popular Jeep Wran-

gler ... just days before announcing official fall hikes averaging 1.9%, or $422.
... Ford says its 1997 model prices were up an average of 1.2%, or $281. ...
But its computations don't include the July 1 [1996] price hikes [ranging up to
$885] on the [two models] which account for a quarter of its U.S. sales. ... In
announcing a boost of 1.7%, or $391 per vehicle, [GM] omitted prices on a
huge crop of overhauled models coming this fall. A GM spokesman says it is
unfair to compare prices on redesigned models . . . with those of previous
models. But dealers say many shoppers don't buy that logic.[2]

You can look at disinformation in the business context as being of
two different types: purposeful and accidental.

PURPOSEFUL BUSINESS DISINFORMATION

In one case, a manufacturing firm was planning to expand its production capacity by building more plants. To do this, it sought to develop joint-venture partners. However, it seemed that it was going to
take time to put all of these planned facilities in place. The company
sought to gain time for its expansion plans to take hold by keeping out
potential competitors until its new capacity was in operation. It also
wished to project a very positive image of its strength and progress to
reassure its current investors and joint venturers, as well as to bring in
new ones. The way this was accomplished was through business
disinformation.

The disinformation was produced by arranging for stories on new
production capacity that overstated the status of new projects. The company did not engage in actual fraud, such as misrepresenting the status of these projects on its books in a material way, so this move was
not illegal. But it was purposeful business disinformation.

Business disinformation is sometimes generated specifically to mislead competitors. For example, in many technology-based industries,
the development of new products and processes is quite costly and
time consuming. That means if you believe that a competitor is significantly ahead of you in a particular area, you might abandon your firm's
work in that area, reasoning that you could never catch up.

For example, to determine the technological positioning of key competitors, companies have routinely used on-line databases to identify
competitors' new patents as they are issued. In some industries, this
practice has reportedly been met by a countermeasure: business
disinformation. Some companies reportedly have even patented "mistakes," that is, developments or compounds with little or no value,
seeking to throw their competitors' tracking and mapping patent activity off the track. One goal is to convince the competitors that the
firm is more highly technologically advanced than it really is, thus dis-
couraging the competitor.

ACCIDENTAL BUSINESS DISINFORMATION

Accidental business disinformation can best be understood by looking at how and where it often develops. Disinformation usually originates from the enterprise itself. For example, in one case, a business firm may have one of its officers give an interview to a local newspaper. The goal of the interview is evidently to improve the firm's community image. During the interview, the reporter's expected questions about the firm, its plans, and its future are answered, with great care, by the officer.

The reporter leaves with notes, quotes, handouts, and impressions. When the article is written, all of these go into the final product. In writing the article, the conclusions drawn by the reporter are not precisely correct. In fact, the officer giving the interview appears to have worked diligently to have the reporter draw certain conclusions about the company's financial and marketing successes without ever having to state them as facts. This enables the reporter, not the officer of the business, to be the source of the now public disinformation.

As the conclusions and statements (not attributed to the officer or the corporation, but merely provided as statements setting the context of the interview), do not disparage or harm the firm, the firm has no incentive to seek a correction.[3]

The article, including its disinformation, then quickly becomes an important input to trade newsletters and newspapers, to investment analysts, and to others following the firm or the industry. In turn, these sources generate a second level of disinformation by repeating the first level of disinformation. The effect is that industry observers indicate that the firm is very successful and well positioned for future growth.

In this case, if the firm did nothing, it would be a case of accidental disinformation. However, it appeared that the firm was hoping to have the article serve to launch this disinformation. It also appeared that the spread of the disinformation was accomplished, in part, by the firm copying and redistributing the original article, thus assisting in its use by others. So even if the initial generation of the disinformation were accidental, the actions of the firm in assuring its dissemination quickly converted it to purposeful disinformation.

This is all very different from letting a competitor make a mistake. There is no obligation on you to quash, contradict, or correct speculation, particularly when it is clearly speculation and you have no response to make.

COSTS AND CONSEQUENCES OF DISINFORMATION

As illustrated, disinformation is already present in the competitive environment. However, that does not mean it is proper. In fact, undertaking disinformation of any type risks significant damages to the business seeking to use it, in addition to its obvious ethical costs. There are four compelling reasons, in addition to the obvious ethical considerations, for avoiding this practice.

First, if pushed too far, disinformation activities can easily cross the line into fraud. In one of the examples noted earlier, the company seeking to make itself look better for joint-venture partners, the disinformation was produced by arranging for stories on new production capacity that overstated the status of new projects. At that point, the company had not engaged in actual fraud. However, in its efforts to maintain the credibility of its deception, the corporation was faced with the necessity to take other steps. Eventually it had to do something with its quarterly reports to investors. There it crossed the line— it misrepresented the status of these projects on its books in a material way. That is, instead of noting that the projects were still under negotiation (which they were), it "booked" them as if they were completed transactions (which they were not). That moved the efforts from disinformation to fraud. The U.S. SEC found out about and disciplined the firm for this fraud. A bright line had been crossed.

Second, for disinformation to work most effectively, your own enterprise must act as if it believes the disinformation. To achieve that, you must, in essence, mislead most if not all of your own people as well as your competitors. Eventually you will pay a price for that— you will suffer *blowback*. Blowback is the contamination of your own intelligence channels or information on which you base your own decisions by the disinformation that you have directed at your competitor. In the business context, it means that your own intelligence and planning personnel (and others as well) are also being misled by your own disinformation.

Third, using disinformation will damage your own credibility. For example, many years ago, IBM was accused of "freezing" competitors by continually announcing the pending release of new products that were not ready for release. The U.S. Department of Justice argued that this practice violated the antitrust laws, since it kept IBM's competitors from being able to sell to the "frozen" accounts. The case was settled with no admission that the practice occurred or that it was illegal. However, years later, in an infamous internal memo, the CEO of IBM excoriated his sales force for failing to work hard enough. Curiously, that same executive had been a sales executive during the era of the alleged freezing. Could low sales morale have been one result of years of selling products which did not appear (i.e., a casualty of disinformation)? One must wonder if the sales force's evident lackadaisical behavior had been impacted by the efforts years before that resulted in the sales force trying to market products that were not available, which they did not know were not available.[4]

Last, disinformation operations may also create an environment which is damaging to the people actually managing the disinformation program. There are anecdotal data suggesting that lying is more stressful than telling the truth.[5]

NOTES

1. Bob Woodward, "U.S. Reportedly Deceived Gadhafi," [Allentown] *Morning Call*, 2 October 1986, A26.

2. "Smoke and Mirrors in Detroit," *Business Week*, 26 August 1996, 30–31.

3. Even if a correction were requested and eventually printed, the damage would have been done. Retractions and corrections rarely catch up with those who read the original story.

4. "At any point in the [marketing communications] process, interfering noise may reduce the effectiveness of the system." W. J. Stanton, *Fundamentals of Marketing*, 2d ed. (New York: McGraw-Hill, 1967), 498.

5. See, for example, Bob Coder, "To Tell the Truth," *Reading* [Pennsylvania] *Eagle/Times*, 15 May 1997, A21.

B

Critical Legislation

OVERVIEW

Due to their importance, we have included the full official texts of two
critical legal documents: the state-level Uniform Trade Secrets Act and
the federal Economic Espionage Act of 1996, which is based on the
UTSA.

To facilitate a better understanding of what each of these does and
does not do, we have also provided supplemental information explaining them. In the case of the UTSA, we have reprinted (with permission) the official comments of those legal experts who actually drafted
the UTSA. In the case of the EEA, we have extracted remarks made
during the U.S. House and Senate proceedings on the law, as well as
the only official section-by-section analysis of the law's intended scope.

UNIFORM TRADE SECRETS ACT
WITH OFFICIAL COMMENTS

UNIFORM TRADE SECRETS ACT
WITH 1985 AMENDMENTS
Drafted by the

NATIONAL CONFERENCE OF COMMISSIONERS
ON UNIFORM STATE LAWS
and by it
Approved and Recommended for Enactment
in All the States
At its
ANNUAL CONFERENCE
MEETING IN ITS NINETY-FOURTH YEAR
IN MINNEAPOLIS, MINNESOTA
AUGUST 2–9, 1985
With Prefatory Note and Comments[1]

* * * *

Final, approved copies of this Act and other printed matter issued by the Conference may be obtained from:

NATIONAL CONFERENCE OF COMMISSIONERS
ON UNIFORM STATE LAWS
676 North St. Clair Street, Suite 1700
Chicago, Illinois 60611
(312) 915–0195 Fax (312) 915–0187
UNIFORM TRADE SECRETS ACT
WITH 1985 AMENDMENTS

TABLE OF CONTENTS

**UNIFORM TRADE SECRETS ACT
WITH 1985 AMENDMENTS**

(The 1985 Amendments are Indicated by Underscore and Strikeout)[2]

PREFATORY NOTE

A valid patent provides a legal monopoly for seventeen years in exchange for public disclosure of an invention. If, however, the courts ultimately decide that the Patent Office improperly issued a patent, an invention will have been disclosed to competitors with no corresponding benefit. In view of the substantial number of patents that are invalidated by the courts, many businesses now elect to protect commercially valuable information through reliance upon the state law of trade secret protection. *Kewanee Oil Co. v. Bicron Corp.*, 416 U.S. 470 (1974), which establishes that neither the Patent Clause of the United States Constitution nor the federal patent laws pre-empt state trade secret protection for patentable or unpatentable information, may well have increased the extent of this reliance.

The recent decision in *Aronson v. Quick Point Pencil Co.*, 99 S.Ct. 1096, 201 USPQ 1 (1979) reaffirmed *Kewanee* and held that federal patent law is not a barrier to a contract in which someone agrees to pay a continuing royalty in exchange for the disclosure of trade secrets concerning a product.

Notwithstanding the commercial importance of state trade secret law to interstate business, this law has not developed satisfactorily. In the first place, its development is uneven. Although there typically are a substantial number of reported decisions in states that are commercial centers, this is not the case in less populous and more agricultural jurisdictions. Secondly, even in states in which there has been significant litigation, there is undue uncertainty concerning the parameters of trade secret protection, and the appropriate remedies for misappropriation of a trade secret. One commentator observed:

> "Under technological and economic pressures, industry continues to rely on trade secret protection despite the doubtful and confused status of both common law and statutory remedies. Clear, uniform trade secret protection is urgently needed. . . ."
>
> Comment, "Theft of Trade Secrets: The Need for a Statutory Solution," 120 U.Pa.L.Rev. 378, 380–81 (1971).

In spite of this need, the most widely accepted rules of trade secret law, § 757 of the Restatement of Torts, were among the sections omitted from the Restatement of Torts, 2d (1978).

The Uniform Act codifies the basic principles of common law trade secret protection, preserving its essential distinctions from patent law. Under both the Act and common law principles, for example, more than one person can be entitled to trade secret protection with respect to the same information, and analysis involving the "reverse engineering" of a lawfully obtained product in order to discover a trade secret is permissible. *Compare* Uniform Act, Section 1(2) (misappropriation means acquisition of a trade secret by means that should be known to be improper and unauthorized disclosure or use of information that one should know is the trade secret of another) *with Miller v. Owens-Illinois, Inc.*, 187 USPQ 47, 48 (D.Md.1975) (alternative holding) (prior, independent discovery a complete defense to liability for misappropriation) *and Wesley-Jessen, Inc., v. Reynolds*, 182 USPQ 135, 144-45, (N.D.Ill.1974) (alternative holding) (unrestricted sale and lease of camera that could be reversed engineered in several days to reveal alleged trade secrets preclude relief for misappropriation).

For liability to exist under this Act, a Section 1(4) trade secret must exist and either a person's acquisition of the trade secret, disclosure of the trade secret to others, or use of the trade secret must be improper under Section 1(2). The mere copying of an unpatented item is not actionable.

Like traditional trade secret law, the Uniform Act contains general concepts. The contribution of the Uniform Act is substitution of unitary definitions of trade secret and trade secret misappropriation, and a single statute of limitations for the various property, quasi-contractual, and violation of fiduciary relationship theories of noncontractual liability utilized at common law. The Uniform Act also codifies the results of the better reasoned cases concerning the remedies for trade secret misappropriation.

*   *   *   *

UNIFORM TRADE SECRETS ACT
WITH 1985 AMENDMENTS

SECTION 1. DEFINITIONS. As used in this [Act], unless the context requires otherwise:

(1) "Improper means" includes theft, bribery, misrepresentation, breach or inducement of a breach of a duty to maintain secrecy, or espionage through electronic or other means;

(2) "Misappropriation" means:

(i) acquisition of a trade secret of another by a person who knows or has reason to know that the trade secret was acquired by improper means; or

(ii) disclosure or use of a trade secret of another without express or implied consent by a person who

(A) used improper means to acquire knowledge of the trade secret; or

(B) at the time of disclosure or use, knew or had reason to know that his knowledge of the trade secret was

(I) derived from or through a person who had utilized improper means to acquire it;

(II) acquired under circumstances giving rise to a duty to maintain its secrecy or limit its use; or

(III) derived from or through a person who owed a duty to the person seeking relief to maintain its secrecy or limit its use; or

(C) before a material change of his [or her] position, knew or had reason to know that it was a trade secret and that knowledge of it had been acquired by accident or mistake.

(3) "Person" means a natural person, corporation, business trust, estate, trust, partnership, association, joint venture, government, governmental subdivision or agency, or any other legal or commercial entity.

(4) "Trade secret" means information, including a formula, pattern, compilation, program, device, method, technique, or process, that:

(i) derives independent economic value, actual or potential, from not being generally known to, and not being readily ascertainable by proper means by, other persons who can obtain economic value from its disclosure or use, and

(ii) is the subject of efforts that are reasonable under the circumstances to maintain its secrecy.

COMMENT[3]

One of the broadly stated policies behind trade secret law is "the maintenance of standards of commercial ethics." Kewanee Oil Co. v. Bicron Corp., 416 U.S. 470 (1974). *The Restatement of Torts, Section 757, Comment (f), notes: "A complete catalogue of improper means is not possible," but Section 1(1) includes a partial listing.*

Proper means include:

1. Discovery by independent invention;

2. Discovery by "reverse engineering," that is, by starting with the known product and working backward to find the method by which it was developed. The acquisition of the known product must, of course, also be by a fair and honest means, such as purchase of the item on the open market for reverse engineering to be lawful;

3. Discovery under a license from the owner of the trade secret;

4. Observation of the item in public use or on public display;

5. Obtaining the trade secret from published literature.

Improper means could include otherwise lawful conduct which is improper under the circumstances; e.g., an airplane overflight used as aerial reconnaissance to determine the competitor's plant layout during construction of the plant. E. I. du Pont de Nemours & Co., Inc. v. Christopher, *431 F.2d 1012 (CA5, 1970), cert. den. 400 U.S. 1024 (1970). Because the trade secret can be destroyed through public knowledge, the unauthorized disclosure of a trade secret is also a misappropriation.*

The type of accident or mistake that can result in a misappropriation under Section 1(2)(ii)(C) involves conduct by a person seeking relief that does not constitute a failure of efforts that are reasonable under the circumstances to maintain its secrecy under Section 1(4)(ii).

The definition of "trade secret" contains a reasonable departure from the Restatement of Torts (First) definition which required that a trade secret be "continuously used in one's business." The broader definition in the proposed Act extends protection to a plaintiff who has not yet had an opportunity or acquired the means to put a trade secret to use. The definition includes information that has commercial value from a negative viewpoint, for example the results of lengthy and expensive research which proves that a certain process will not work could be of great value to a competitor.

Cf. Telex Corp. v. IBM Corp., *510 F.2d 894 (CA10, 1975) per curiam, cert. dismissed 423 U.S. 802 (1975) (liability imposed for developmental cost savings with respect to product not marketed). Because a trade secret need not be exclusive to confer a competitive advantage, different independent developers can acquire rights in the same trade secret.*

The words "method, technique" are intended to include the concept of "know-how."

The language "not being generally known to and not being readily ascertainable by proper means by other persons" does not require that information be generally known to the public for trade secret rights to be lost. If the principal persons who can obtain economic benefit from information are aware of it, there is no trade secret. A method of casting metal, for example, may be unknown to the general public but readily known within the foundry industry.

Information is readily ascertainable if it is available in trade journals, reference books, or published materials. Often, the nature of a product lends itself to being readily copied as soon as it is available on the market. On the other hand, if reverse engineering is lengthy and expensive, a person who discovers the trade secret through reverse engineering can have a trade secret in the information obtained from reverse engineering.

Finally, reasonable efforts to maintain secrecy have been held to include advising employees of the existence of a trade secret, limiting access to a trade secret on "need to know basis," and controlling plant access. On the other hand, public disclosure of information through display, trade journal publications, advertising, or other carelessness can preclude protection.

The efforts required to maintain secrecy are those "reasonable under the circumstances." The courts do not require that extreme and unduly expensive procedures be taken to protect trade secrets against flagrant industrial espionage. See E. I. du Pont de Nemours & Co., Inc. v. Christopher, *supra. It follows that reasonable use of a trade secret including controlled disclosure to employees and licensees is consistent with the requirement of relative secrecy.*

SECTION 2. INJUNCTIVE RELIEF.

(a) Actual or threatened misappropriation may be enjoined. Upon application to the court, an injunction shall be terminated when the trade secret has ceased to exist, but the injunction may be continued for an additional reasonable period of time in order to eliminate commercial advantage that otherwise would be derived from the misappropriation.

(b) In exceptional circumstances, an injunction may condition future use upon payment of a reasonable royalty for no longer than the period of time for which use could have been prohibited. Exceptional circumstances include, but are not limited to, a material and prejudicial change of position prior to acquiring knowledge or reason to know of misappropriation that renders a prohibitive injunction inequitable.

(c) In appropriate circumstances, affirmative acts to protect a trade secret may be compelled by court order.

COMMENT

Injunctions restraining future use and disclosure of misappropriated trade secrets frequently are sought. Although punitive perpetual injunctions have been granted, e.g., Elcor Chemical Corp. v. Agri-Sul, Inc., 494 S.W.2d 204 *(Tex.Civ.App.1973), Section 2(a) of this Act adopts the position of the trend of authority limiting the duration of injunctive relief to the extent of the temporal advantage over good faith competitors gained by a misappropriation. See,* e.g., K-2 Ski Co. v. Head Ski Co., Inc., 506 F.2d 471 (CA9, 1974) *(maximum appropriate duration of both temporary and permanent injunctive relief is period of time it would have taken defendant to discover trade secrets lawfully through either independent development or reverse engineering of plaintiff's products).*

The general principle of Section 2(a) and (b) is that an injunction should last for as long as is necessary, but no longer than is necessary, to eliminate the commercial advantage or "lead time" with respect to good faith competitors that a person has obtained through misappropriation. Subject to any additional period of restraint necessary to negate lead time, an injunction accordingly should terminate when a former trade secret becomes either generally known to good faith competitors or generally knowable to them because of the lawful availability of products that can be reverse engineered to reveal a trade secret.

For example, assume that A has a valuable trade secret of which B and C, the other industry members, are originally unaware. If B subsequently misap-

propriates the trade secret and is enjoined from use, but C later lawfully reverse engineers the trade secret, the injunction restraining B is subject to termination as soon as B's lead time has been dissipated. All of the persons who could derive economic value from use of the information are now aware of it, and there is no longer a trade secret under Section 1(4). It would be anticompetitive to continue to restrain B after any lead time that B had derived from misappropriation had been removed.

If a misappropriator either has not taken advantage of lead time or good faith competitors already have caught up with a misappropriator at the time that a case is decided, future disclosure and use of a former trade secret by a misappropriator will not damage a trade secret owner and no injunctive restraint of future disclosure and use is appropriate. See, e.g., Northern Petrochemical Co. v. Tomlinson, *484 F.2d 1057 (CA7, 1973) (affirming trial court's denial of preliminary injunction in part because an explosion at its plant prevented an alleged misappropriator from taking advantage of lead time);* Kubik, Inc. v. Hull, *185 USPQ 391 (Mich.App.1974) (discoverability of trade secret by lawful reverse engineering made by injunctive relief punitive rather than compensatory).*

Section 2(b) deals with the special situation in which future use by a misappropriator will damage a trade secret owner but an injunction against future use nevertheless is inappropriate due to exceptional circumstances. Exceptional circumstances include the existence of an overriding public interest which requires the denial of a prohibitory injunction against future damaging use and a person's reasonable reliance upon acquisition of a misappropriated trade secret in good faith and without reason to know of its prior misappropriation that would be prejudiced by a prohibitory injunction against future damaging use. Republic Aviation Corp. v. Schenk, *152 USPQ 830 (N.Y.Sup.Ct.1967) illustrates the public interest justification for withholding prohibitory injunctive relief. The court considered that enjoining a misappropriator from supplying the U.S. with an aircraft weapons control system would have endangered military personnel in Viet Nam. The prejudice to a good faith third party justification for withholding prohibitory injunctive relief can arise upon a trade secret owner's notification to a good faith third party that the third party has knowledge of a trade secret as a result of misappropriation by another. This notice suffices to make the third party a misappropriator thereafter under Section 1(2)(ii)(B)(I). In weighing an aggrieved person's interests and the interests of a third party who has relied in good faith upon his or her ability to utilize information, a court may conclude that restraining future use of the information by the third party is unwarranted. With respect to innocent acquirers of misappropriated trade secrets, Section 2(b) is consistent with the principle of 4 Restatement Torts (First) § 758(b) (1939), but rejects the Restatement's literal conferral of absolute immunity upon all third parties who have paid value in good faith for a trade secret misappropriated by another. The position taken by the Uni-*

form Act is supported by Forest Laboratories, Inc. v. Pillsbury Co., *452 F.2d 621 (CA7, 1971) in which a defendant's purchase of assets of a corporation to which a trade secret had been disclosed in confidence was not considered to confer immunity upon the defendant.*

When Section 2(b) applies, a court has discretion to substitute an injunction conditioning future use upon payment of a reasonable royalty for an injunction prohibiting future use. Like all injunctive relief for misappropriation, a royalty order injunction is appropriate only if a misappropriator has obtained a competitive advantage through misappropriation and only for the duration of that competitive advantage. In some situations, typically those involving good faith acquirers of trade secrets misappropriated by others, a court may conclude that the same considerations that render a prohibitory injunction against future use inappropriate also render a royalty order injunction inappropriate. See, generally, Prince Manufacturing, Inc. v. Automatic Partner, Inc., *198 USPQ 618 (N.J.Super.Ct.1976) (purchaser of misappropriator's assets from receiver after trade secret disclosed to public through sale of product not subject to liability for misappropriation).*

A royalty order injunction under Section 2(b) should be distinguished from a reasonable royalty alternative measure of damages under Section 3(a). See the Comment to Section 3 for discussion of the differences in the remedies.

Section 2(c) authorizes mandatory injunctions requiring that a misappropriator return the fruits of misappropriation to an aggrieved person, e.g., the return of stolen blueprints or the surrender of surreptitious photographs or recordings.

Where more than one person is entitled to trade secret protection with respect to the same information, only that one from whom misappropriation occurred is entitled to a remedy.

SECTION 3. DAMAGES.

(a) Except to the extent that a material and prejudicial change of position prior to acquiring knowledge or reason to know of misappropriation renders a monetary recovery inequitable, a complainant is entitled to recover damages for misappropriation. Damages can include both the actual loss caused by misappropriation and the unjust enrichment caused by misappropriation that is not taken into account in computing actual loss. In lieu of damages measured by any other methods, the damages caused by misappropriation may be measured by imposition of liability for a reasonable royalty for a misappropriator's unauthorized disclosure or use of a trade secret.

(b) If willful and malicious misappropriation exists, the court may award exemplary damages in an amount not exceeding twice any award made under subsection (a).

COMMENT

Like injunctive relief, a monetary recovery for trade secret misappropriation is appropriate only for the period in which information is entitled to protection as a trade secret, plus the additional period, if any, in which a misappropriator retains an advantage over good faith competitors because of misappropriation. Actual damage to a complainant and unjust benefit to a misappropriator are caused by misappropriation during this time alone. See Conmar Products Corp. v. Universal Slide Fastener Co., *172 F.2d 150 (CA2, 1949) (no remedy for period subsequent to disclosure of trade secret by issued patent);* Carboline Co. v. Jarboe, *454 S.W.2d 540 (Mo.1970) (recoverable monetary relief limited to period that it would have taken misappropriator to discover trade secret without misappropriation). A claim for actual damages and net profits can be combined with a claim for injunctive relief, but, if both claims are granted, the injunctive relief ordinarily will preclude a monetary award for a period in which the injunction is effective.*

As long as there is no double counting, Section 3(a) adopts the principle of the recent cases allowing recovery of both a complainant's actual losses and a misappropriator's unjust benefit that are caused by misappropriation. E.g., Tri-Tron International v. Velto, *525 F.2d 432 (CA9, 1975) (complainant's loss and misappropriator's benefit can be combined). Because certain cases may have sanctioned double counting in a combined award of losses and unjust benefit, e.g.,* Telex Corp. v. IBM Corp., *510 F.2d 894 (CA10, 1975) (per curiam), cert. dismissed, 423 U.S. 802 (1975) (IBM recovered rentals lost due to displacement by misappropriator's products without deduction for expenses saved by displacement; as a result of rough approximations adopted by the trial judge, IBM also may have recovered developmental costs saved by misappropriator through misappropriation with respect to the same customers), the Act adopts an express prohibition upon the counting of the same item as both a loss to a complainant and an unjust benefit to a misappropriator.*

As an alternative to all other methods of measuring damages caused by a misappropriator's past conduct, a complainant can request that damages be based upon a demonstrably reasonable royalty for a misappropriator's unauthorized disclosure or use of a trade secret. In order to justify this alternative measure of damages, there must be competent evidence of the amount of a reasonable royalty.

The reasonable royalty alternative measure of damages for a misappropriator's past conduct under Section 3(a) is readily distinguishable from a Section 2(b) royalty order injunction, which conditions a misappropriator's future ability to use a trade secret upon payment of a reasonable royalty. A Section 2(b) royalty order injunction is appropriate only in exceptional circumstances; whereas a reasonable royalty measure of damages is a general option. Because Section 3(a) damages are awarded for a misappropriator's past conduct and a Section 2(b) royalty order injunction regulates a misappropriator's future conduct, both remedies cannot be awarded for the same conduct. If a royalty order injunction is appropriate because of a person's material and prejudicial change of position prior to having reason to know that a trade secret has been acquired from a misappropriator, damages, moreover, should not be awarded for past conduct that occurred prior to notice that a misappropriated trade secret has been acquired.

Monetary relief can be appropriate whether or not injunctive relief is granted under Section 2. If a person charged with misappropriation has materially and prejudicially changed position in reliance upon knowledge of a trade secret acquired in good faith and without reason to know of its misappropriation by another, however, the same considerations that can justify denial of all injunctive relief also can justify denial of all monetary relief. See Conmar Products Corp. v. Universal Slide Fastener Co., 172 F.2d 1950 (CA2, 1949) *(no relief against new employer of employee subject to contractual obligation not to disclose former employer's trade secrets where new employer innocently had committed $40,000 to develop the trade secrets prior to notice of misappropriation).*

If willful and malicious misappropriation is found to exist, Section 3(b) authorizes the court to award a complainant exemplary damages in addition to the actual recovery under Section 3(a) an amount not exceeding twice that recovery. This provision follows federal patent law in leaving discretionary trebling to the judge even though there may be a jury, compare 35 U.S.C. Section 284 (1976).

Whenever more than one person is entitled to trade secret protection with respect to the same information, only that one from whom misappropriation occurred is entitled to a remedy.

SECTION 4. ATTORNEY'S FEES.

If

(i) a claim of misappropriation is made in bad faith,
(ii) a motion to terminate an injunction is made or resisted in bad faith, or
(iii) willful and malicious misappropriation exists,

the court may award reasonable attorney's fees to the prevailing party.

COMMENT

Section 4 allows a court to award reasonable attorney fees to a prevailing party in specified circumstances as a deterrent to specious claims of misappropriation, to specious efforts by a misappropriator to terminate injunctive relief, and to willful and malicious misappropriation. In the latter situation, the court should take into consideration the extent to which a complainant will recover exemplary damages in determining whether additional attorney's fees should be awarded. Again, patent law is followed in allowing the judge to determine whether attorney's fees should be awarded even if there is a jury, compare 35 U.S.C. Section 285 (1976).

SECTION 5. PRESERVATION OF SECRECY.

In an action under this [Act], a court shall preserve the secrecy of an alleged trade secret by reasonable means, which may include granting protective orders in connection with discovery proceedings, holding in-camera hearings, sealing the records of the action, and ordering any person involved in the litigation not to disclose an alleged trade secret without prior court approval.

COMMENT

If reasonable assurances of maintenance of secrecy could not be given, meritorious trade secret litigation would be chilled. In fashioning safeguards of confidentiality, a court must ensure that a respondent is provided sufficient information to present a defense and a trier of fact sufficient information to resolve the merits. In addition to the illustrative techniques specified in the statute, courts have protected secrecy in these cases by restricting disclosures to a party's counsel and his or her assistants and by appointing a disinterested expert as a special master to hear secret information and report conclusions to the court.

SECTION 6. STATUTE OF LIMITATIONS.

An action for misappropriation must be brought within 3 years after the misappropriation is discovered or by the exercise of reasonable diligence should have been discovered. For the purposes of this section, a continuing misappropriation constitutes a single claim.

COMMENT

There presently is a conflict of authority as to whether trade secret misappropriation is a continuing wrong. Compare Monolith Portland Midwest Co. v. Kaiser Aluminum & Chemical Corp., 407 F.2d 288 (CA9, 1969) *(not a continuing wrong under California law—limitation period upon all recovery begins upon initial misappropriation) with* Underwater Storage, Inc. v. U. S. Rubber Co., 371 F.2d 950 (CADC, 1966), cert. den., 386 U.S. 911 (1967) *(continuing wrong under general principles—limitation period* with respect to a specific act of misappropriation begins at the time that the act of misappropriation occurs).

This Act rejects a continuing wrong approach to the statute of limitations but delays the commencement of the limitation period until an aggrieved person discovers or reasonably should have discovered the existence of misappropriation. If objectively reasonable notice of misappropriation exists, three years is sufficient time to vindicate one's legal rights.

SECTION 7. EFFECT ON OTHER LAW.

(a) Except as provided in subsection (b), this [Act] displaces conflicting tort, restitutionary, and other law of this State providing civil remedies for misappropriation of a trade secret.

(b) This [Act] does not affect:

(1) contractual remedies, whether or not based upon misappropriation of a trade secret;

(2) other civil remedies that are not based upon misappropriation of a trade secret; or

(3) criminal remedies, whether or not based upon misappropriation of a trade secret.

COMMENT

This Act does not deal with criminal remedies for trade secret misappropriation and is not a comprehensive statement of civil remedies. It applies to a duty to protect competitively significant secret information that is imposed by law. It does not apply to a duty voluntarily assumed through an express or an implied-in-fact contract. The enforceability of covenants not to disclose trade secrets and covenants not to compete that are intended to protect trade secrets, for example, is governed by other law. The Act also does not apply to a duty imposed by law that is not dependent upon the existence of competitively significant secret information, like an agent's duty of loyalty to his or her principal.

SECTION 8. UNIFORMITY OF APPLICATION AND CONSTRUCTION.

This [Act] shall be applied and construed to effectuate its general purpose to make uniform the law with respect to the subject of this [Act] among states enacting it.

SECTION 9. SHORT TITLE.

This [Act] may be cited as the Uniform Trade Secrets Act.

SECTION 10. SEVERABILITY.

If any provision of this [Act] or its application to any person or circumstances is held invalid, the invalidity does not affect other provisions or applications of the [Act] which can be given effect without the invalid provision or application, and to this end the provisions of this [Act] are severable.

SECTION 11. TIME OF TAKING EFFECT.

This [Act] takes effect on _____, and does not apply to misappropriation occurring prior to the effective date. With respect to a continuing misappropriation that began prior to the effective date, the [Act] also does not apply to the continuing misappropriation that occurs after the effective date.

COMMENT

The Act applies exclusively to misappropriation that begins after its effective date. Neither misappropriation that began and ended before the effective date nor misappropriation that began before the effective date and continued thereafter is subject to the Act.

SECTION 12. REPEAL.

The following Acts and parts of Acts are repealed:
(1)
(2)
(3)

ECONOMIC ESPIONAGE ACT OF 1996

"PUBLIC LAW 104-294 – Oct. 11, 1996 – 110 Stat. 3488

"ECONOMIC ESPIONAGE ACT OF 1996

"**An Act to Amend title 18, United States Code, to protect proprietary economic information, and for other purposes.**
"*Be it enacted by the Senate and House of Representatives of the United States of America in Congress assembled,*

"**TITLE I—PROTECTION OF TRADE SECRETS**

"SEC. 101. PROTECTION OF TRADE SECRETS.

(a) IN GENERAL—Title 18, United States Code, is amended by inserting after chapter 89 the following:

'CHAPTER 90—PROTECTION OF TRADE SECRETS

'Sec.
'1831. Economic espionage.
'1832. Theft of trade secrets.
'1833. Exceptions to prohibitions.
'1834. Criminal forfeiture.
'1835. Orders to preserve confidentiality.
'1836. Civil proceedings to enjoin violations.
'1837. Conduct outside the United States.
'1838. Construction with other laws.
'1839. Definitions.

'Sec. 1831. Economic espionage

'(a) IN GENERAL- Whoever, intending or knowing that the offense will benefit any foreign government, foreign instrumentality, or foreign agent, knowingly—
'(1) steals, or without authorization appropriates, takes, carries away, or conceals, or by fraud, artifice, or deception obtains a trade secret;
'(2) without authorization copies, duplicates, sketches, draws, photographs, downloads, uploads, alters, destroys, photocopies, replicates, transmits, delivers, sends, mails, communicates, or conveys a trade secret;
'(3) receives, buys, or possesses a trade secret, knowing the same to have been stolen or appropriated, obtained, or converted without authorization;
'(4) attempts to commit any offense described in any of paragraphs (1) through (3); or

'(5) conspires with one or more other persons to commit any offense described in any of paragraphs (1) through (3), and one or more of such persons do any act to effect the object of the conspiracy,
shall, except as provided in subsection (b), be fined not more than $500,000 or imprisoned not more than 15 years, or both.

'(b) ORGANIZATIONS-Any organization that commits any offense described in subsection (a) shall be fined not more than $10,000,000.

'Sec. 1832. Theft of trade secrets

'(a) Whoever, with intent to convert a trade secret, that is related to or included in a product that is produced for or placed in interstate or foreign commerce, to the economic benefit of anyone other than the owner thereof, and intending or knowing that the offense will, injure any owner of that trade secret, knowingly—

'(1) steals, or without authorization appropriates, takes, carries away, or conceals, or by fraud, artifice, or deception obtains such information;

'(2) without authorization copies, duplicates, sketches, draws, photographs, downloads, uploads, alters, destroys, photocopies, replicates, transmits, delivers, sends, mails, communicates, or conveys such information;

'(3) receives, buys, or possesses such information, knowing the same to have been stolen or appropriated, obtained, or converted without authorization;

'(4) attempts to commit any offense described in paragraphs (1) through (3); or

'(5) conspires with one or more other persons to commit any offense described in paragraphs (1) through (3), and one or more of such persons do any act to effect the object of the conspiracy, shall, except as provided in subsection (b), be fined under this title or imprisoned not more than 10 years, or both.

'(b) Any organization that commits any offense described in subsection (a) shall be fined not more than $5,000,000.

'Sec. 1833. Exceptions to prohibitions

'This chapter does not prohibit—

'(1) any otherwise lawful activity conducted by a governmental entity of the United States, a State, or a political subdivision of a State; or

'(2) the reporting of a suspected violation of law to any governmental entity of the United States, a State, or a political subdivision of a State, if such entity has lawful authority with respect to that violation.

'Sec. 1834. Criminal forfeiture

'(a) The court, in imposing sentence on a person for a violation of this chapter, shall order, in addition to any other sentence imposed, that the person forfeit to the United States—

'(1) any property constituting, or derived from, any proceeds the person obtained, directly or indirectly, as the result of such violation; and

'(2) any of the person's property used, or intended to be used, in any manner or part, to commit or facilitate the commission of such violation, if the court in its discretion so determines, taking into consideration the nature, scope, and proportionality of the use of the property in the offense.

'(b) Property subject to forfeiture under this section, any seizure and disposition thereof, and any administrative or judicial proceeding in relation thereto, shall be governed by section 413 of the Comprehensive Drug Abuse Prevention and Control Act of 1970 (21 U.S.C. 853), except for subsections (d) and (j) of such section, which shall not apply to forfeitures under this section.

'Sec. 1835. Orders to preserve confidentiality

'In any prosecution or other proceeding under this chapter, the court shall enter such orders and take such other action as may be necessary and appropriate to preserve the confidentiality of trade secrets, consistent with the requirements of the Federal Rules of Criminal and Civil Procedure, the Federal Rules of Evidence, and all other applicable laws. An interlocutory appeal by the United States shall lie from a decision or order of a district court authorizing or directing the disclosure of any trade secret.

'Sec. 1836. Civil proceedings to enjoin violations

'(a) The Attorney General may, in a civil action, obtain appropriate injunctive relief against any violation of this section.

'(b) The district courts of the United States shall have exclusive original jurisdiction of civil actions under this subsection.

'Sec. 1837. Applicability to conduct outside the United States

This chapter also applies to conduct occurring outside the United States if—

'(1) the offender is a natural person who is a citizen or permanent resident alien of the United States, or an organization organized under the laws of the United States or a State or political subdivision thereof; or

'(2) an act in furtherance of the offense was committed in the United States.

'Sec. 1838. Construction with other laws

'This chapter shall not be construed to preempt or displace any other remedies, whether civil or criminal, provided by United States Federal, State, commonwealth, possession, or territory law for the misappropriation of a trade secret, or to affect the otherwise lawful disclosure of information by any Government employee under section 552 of title 5 (commonly known as the Freedom of Information Act).

'Sec. 1839. Definitions

'As used in this chapter—

'(1) the term 'foreign instrumentality' means any agency, bureau, ministry, component, institution, association, or any legal, commercial, or business organization, corporation, firm, or entity that is substantially owned, controlled, sponsored, commanded, managed, or dominated by a foreign government;

'(2) the term 'foreign agent' means any officer, employee, proxy, servant, delegate, or representative of a foreign government;

'(3) the term 'trade secret' means all forms and types of financial, business, scientific, technical, economic, or engineering information, including patterns, plans, compilations, program devices, formulas, designs, prototypes, methods, techniques, processes, procedures, programs, or codes, whether tangible or intangible, and whether or how stored, compiled, or memorialized physically, electronically, graphically, photographically, or in writing if—

'(A) the owner thereof has taken reasonable measures to keep such information secret; and

'(B) the information derives independent economic value, actual or potential, from not being generally known to, and not being readily ascertainable through proper means by, the public; and

'(4) the term 'owner', with respect to a trade secret, means the person or entity in whom or in which rightful legal or equitable title to, or license in, the trade secret is reposed.'.

(b) CLERICAL AMENDMENT— [omitted]

(c) REPORTS—Not later than 2 years and 4 years after the date of the enactment of this Act, the Attorney General shall report to Congress on the amounts received and distributed from fines for offenses under this chapter deposited in the Crime Victims Fund established by section 1402 of the Victims of Crime Act of 1984 (42 U.S.C. 10601).

SEC. 102. WIRE AND ELECTRONIC COMMUNICATIONS INTERCEPTION AND INTERCEPTION OF ORAL COMMUNICATIONS.

Section 2516(1)(c) of title 18, United States Code, is amended by inserting 'chapter 90 (relating to protection of trade secrets),' after 'chapter 37 (relating to espionage),'.

[text of following titles omitted:
- Title II—National Information Infrastructure Protection Act of 1996;
- Title III—Transfer of Persons Found Not Guilty By Reason of Insanity;
- Title IV—Establishment of Boys and Girls Clubs'
- Title V—Use of Certain Technology to Facilitate Criminal Conduct; and
- Title VI—Technical and Minor Amendments]

SELECTED CONGRESSIONAL REMARKS ON THE ECONOMIC ESPIONAGE ACT OF 1996

US House of Representatives—
Sept. 17, 1996 (104 Cong. Rec. p. H10462)

"[S]ome Members thought that this legislation might inhibit common and acceptable business practices. For example, employees who leave one company to work for another naturally take their general knowledge and experience with them and no one, no one wishes to see them penalized as a result. Similarly, reverse engineering is an entirely legitimate practice.

"Our bill was carefully drafted to avoid this problem. The very high intent requirements and the narrow definition of a trade secret make it clear that we are talking about extraordinary theft, not mere competition."

US Senate—
Sept. 18, 1996 (104 Cong. Rec. pp. S12213-14)

"REVERSE ENGINEERING

"Some people have asked how this legislation might affect reverse engineering. Reverse engineering is a broad term that encompasses a variety of actions. The important thing is to focus on whether the accused has committed one of the prohibited acts of this statute rather than whether he or she has 'reverse engineered.' If someone has lawfully gained access to a trade secret and can replicate it without violating copyright, patent or this law, then that form of 'reverse engineering' should be fine. For example, if a person can drink Coca-Cola and, because he happens to have highly refined taste buds, can figure out what the formula is, then this legislation cannot be used against him. Likewise, if a person can look at a product and, by using their own general skills and expertise, dissect the necessary attributes of the product, then that person should be free from any threat of prosecution.

"DEFINITION OF TRADE SECRETS

"Unlike patented material, something does not have to be novel or inventive, in the patent law sense, in order to be a trade secret. Of course, often it will be because an owner will have a patented invention that he or she has chosen to maintain the material as a trade secret rather than reveal it through the patent process. Even if the material is not novel in the patent law sense, some form of novelty is probably inevitable since 'that which does not possess novelty is usually known; secrecy, in the context of trade secrets implies at least minimal novelty.' Kewanee Oil Co., 416 U.S. at 476. While we do not strictly impose a novelty or inventiveness requirement in order for material to be considered a trade secret, looking at the novelty or uniqueness of a piece of information or knowledge should inform courts in determining whether something is a matter of general knowledge, skill or experience.

"Although we do not require novelty or inventiveness, the definition of a trade secret includes the provision that an owner have taken reasonable measures under the circumstances to keep the information confidential. We do not with this definition impose any requirements on companies or owners. Each owner must assess the value of the material it seeks to protect, the extent of a threat of theft, and the ease of theft in determining how extensive their protective measures should be. We anticipate that what constitutes reasonable measures in one particular field of knowledge or industry may vary significantly from what is reasonable in another field or industry. However, some common sense measures are likely to be common across the board. For example, it is only natural that an owner would restrict access to a trade secret to the people who actually need to use the information. It is only natural also that an owner clearly indicate in some form or another that the information is proprietary. However, owners need not take heroic or extreme measures in order for their efforts to be reasonable.

"GENERAL KNOWLEDGE NOT COVERED BY DEFINITION OF TRADE SECRETS

"In the course of reconciling the Senate and House versions of this legislation, we eliminated the portion of the definition of trade secret that indicated that general knowledge, skills and experience were not included in the meaning of that term. Its elimination from the statutory language does not mean that general knowledge can be a trade secret. Rather, we believed that the definition of trade secrets in itself cannot include general knowledge. Thus, it was unnecessary and redundant to both define what does and what does not constitute a trade secret.

"Our reason initially for putting the exception in was to state as clearly as possible that this legislation does not apply to innocent innovators or to individuals who seek to capitalize on their lawfully developed knowledge skill or abilities. Employees, for example, who change employers or start their own companies should be able to apply their talents without fear of prosecution because two safeguards against overreaching are built into the law."

SECTION-BY-SECTION ANALYSIS[4]

"Section 1. TITLE.—Section 1 states the short title of the bill as the "Economic Espionage Act of 1996."

"Section 2. PROTECTION OF TRADE SECRETS. This section adds a new section to Chapter 31 of Title 18 of the United States Code. The new section, section 670,[5] creates the crime of wrongfully copying or otherwise controlling a trade secret.

"Section 670(a)—Offense.—Subsection (a) of new section 670 creates the criminal offense involving the misappropriation of trade secrets. The offense provides that anyone who 'wrongfully copies or otherwise controls' a trade secret, or attempts or conspires to do so, shall be punished in accordance with subsection (b) of that section. In order for a violation of the statute to be proven, the government must also prove that the defendant committed the offense either (1) with the intent to, or with reason to believe that the offense would, benefit any foreign government, foreign instrumentality, or foreign agent, or (2) with the intent to divert a trade secret related to, or included in, a product that is produced for, or placed in, interstate or foreign commerce, to the use or benefit of anyone other than the owner of the trade secret and with the further intent to, or with reason to believe that the offense would, disadvantage the owner of that trade secret.

"This section punishes the theft, unauthorized appropriation or conversion, duplication, alteration, or destruction of a trade secret. This section is intended to cover both traditional instances of theft, where the object of the crime is removed from the rightful owner's control, as well as non-traditional methods of misappropriation or destruction that involve duplication or alteration. When these nontraditional methods are used the original property never leaves the control of the rightful owner, but the unauthorized duplication or misappropriation effectively destroys the value of what is left with the rightful owner. Given the increased use of electronic information systems, information can now be stolen without transportation and the original usually remains intact. The intent of this statute, therefore, is to ensure that the theft of intangible information is prohibited in the same way that the theft of physical items is punished.

"This section requires that the government prove that the person charged with the crime acted with the intent to accomplish one of two goals. One, a person will be guilty under this section if they wrongfully copied or otherwise controlled a trade secret with the intent to benefit any foreign government, foreign instrumentality or foreign agent. In this instance, 'benefit' is intended to be interpreted broadly. The defendant did not have to intend to confer an economic benefit to the foreign government, instrumentality, or agent, to himself, or to any third person. Rather, the government need only prove that the actor intended that his actions in copying or otherwise controlling the trade secret would benefit the foreign government, instrumentality, or agent in any way. Therefore, in this circumstance, benefit means not only an economic benefit but also reputational, strategic, or tactical benefit.

"Alternatively, the government may prove that the defendant intended the misappropriated trade secret to be used for the economic benefit of a person other than the rightful owner (which can be the defendant or some other person or entity). In this situation (i.e., when the defendant does not act with the intent to benefit a foreign government, instrumentality, or agent) the government must prove that the defendant intended to confer an economic benefit, not an abstract benefit or reputational enhancement, through his actions. Therefore, a person who discloses a trade secret but who does not intend to gain economically from it, or intends that some other person economically gain from trade secret, cannot be prosecuted under this section. Additionally, when the defendant does not act with the intent to benefit a foreign government, instrumentality or agent, the government must also show that the defendant intended to disadvantage the rightful owner of the information. This additional provision does not require the government to prove malice or evil intent, but merely that the actor knew or was aware to a practical certainty that his conduct would cause some disadvantage to the rightful owner.

"While the term 'wrongfully' is not defined in the statute specifically, the use of the term in this section involves the defendant's knowledge that his or her actions in copying or otherwise exerting control over the information in question was inappropriate. It is not necessary that the government prove that the defendant knew his or her actions were illegal, rather the government must prove that the defendant's actions were not authorized by the nature of his or her relationship to the owner of the property and that the defendant knew or should have known that fact.

"Section 670—PUNISHMENT.—The bill provides for several types of punishment, including fines, imprisonment, or both. The maximum term of incarceration varies depending upon the intent of the person convicted of the crime. If the defendant's intent was to benefit a foreign government, foreign instrumentality, or foreign agent the maximum term of imprisonment is 25 years. In all other cases, the maximum term of imprisonment is 15 years.

"If an organization commits an offense under the section, the maximum fine amount is substantially increased from that otherwise provided under title 18. If an organization commits an offense involving an intent to benefit a foreign government, foreign instrumentality, or foreign agent the maximum fine which may be imposed is $10 million. In all other circumstances, the maximum fine which may be imposed on an organization violating section 670 is $5 million.

"Subsection (c)—DEFINITIONS.—Subsection (c) of new section 670 provides for definitions of some of the key terms used in the section. The definition of the term 'trade secret' is based largely on the definition of that term in the Uniform Trade Secrets Act. As defined in H.R. 3723, 'trade secret' means 'all forms and types of financial, business, scientific, technical, economic, or engineering information' if certain conditions exist, as discussed below. This information includes patterns, plans, compilations, program devices, formulas, designs, prototypes, methods, techniques, processes, procedures, programs, or codes, whether such properties are tangible or intangible, and regardless of the means by which such property is stored or compiled, or memorialized physically, electronically, graphically, photographically, or in writing. These general categories of information are included in the definition of trade secret for illustrative purposes and should not be read to limit the definition of trade secret. It is the Committee's intent that this definition be read broadly.

"As defined in the bill, however, in order for information to meet the definition of trade secret, two conditions must be proven to have existed at the time the defendant copied or otherwise exerted control over the information. First, the owner of the information must have taken reasonable measures to keep such information secret. Secret in this context means that the information was not generally known to the public or to the business, scientific, or educational community in which the owner might seek to use the information. The bill requires the owner to take only 'reasonable' measures to keep such information secret. The fact that the owner did not exhaust every conceivable means by which the information could be kept secure does not mean that the information does not satisfy this requirement. Rather, a determination of the 'reasonableness' of the steps taken by the owner to keep the information secret will vary from case to case and be dependent upon the nature of the information in question.

"The definition of trade secret also requires that the information in question derive independent economic value, whether actual or potential, from the fact that the information is not generally known to, and not readily ascertainable through proper means by, the public. Therefore, information which is generally known to the public, or which the public can readily ascertain through proper means, does not satisfy the definition of trade secret under this section.

"The term 'owner' is defined to include the person or entity in whom or in which rightful legal or equitable title to, or license in, the trade secret in reposed. In this case, owner includes both natural persons as well as organizations (such as corporations and partnerships) entitled to own property. It also includes federal, state, and local government organizations, as well as foreign government organizations.

"Subsection (d)—CRIMINAL FORFEITURE.—This section is designed to permit forfeiture of both the proceeds and assets used to facilitate the commission of the offense described in the bill. This section requires that any person convicted of a violation of section 670 shall forfeit all property constituting, or derived from, any proceeds the person obtained as the result of such violation, regardless of whether the proceeds were obtained directly or indirectly from the criminal conduct. This section also requires that the person convicted of violating section 670 forfeit any of the person's property used, or intended to be used, to commit or facilitate the crime. But this section further provides, however, that in determining the extent of the property to be forfeited, the court may take into consideration the nature, scope, and proportionality of the use of the property in the offense. The intent of this proviso is to minimize the number of instances in which the property forfeited is disproportionate to the harm caused by the defendant's conduct.

"The forfeiture provision supplements, and is in addition to, the authorized punishments in the bill. The subsection incorporates existing law that sets forth procedures to be used in the detention, seizure, forfeiture, and ultimate disposition of property forfeited under this subsection.

"Subsection (e)—ORDERS TO PRESERVE CONFIDENTIALITY.— This subsection authorizes the court to preserve the confidentiality of alleged trade secrets during legal proceedings consistent with existing rules of criminal procedure, civil procedure, and evidence, and other applicable laws. The intent of this section is to preserve the confidential nature of the information and, hence, its value. Without such a provision, owners may be reluctant to cooperate in prosecutions for fear of further exposing their trade secrets to public view, thus further devaluing or even destroying their worth.

"Subsection (f)—CIVIL PROCEEDINGS TO ENJOIN VIOLATIONS.— This section empowers the Attorney General to commence a civil action in the United States District Courts to obtain injunctive relief against a violation of new section 670. The standards for obtaining such injunctive relief are to be those provided for under the Federal Rules of Civil Procedure. The district courts shall have exclusive jurisdiction over actions brought under this subsection. This subsection is neither intended to create a general civil cause of action nor does it authorize persons other than the Attorney General to commence a civil action to enjoin a violation of section 670.

"Subsection (g)—TERRITORIAL APPLICATION.—To rebut the general presumption against the extraterritoriality of U.S. criminal laws, this subsection makes it clear that the Act is meant to apply to the specified conduct occurring beyond U.S. borders. To ensure that there is some nexus between the ascertaining of such jurisdiction and the offense, however, extraterritorial jurisdiction exists only if the offender is a United States citizen or permanent resident alien, an organization substantially owned or controlled by United States citizens or permanent resident aliens, or is incorporated in the United States. Alternatively, extraterritorial jurisdiction will exist if an act in furtherance of the offense was committed in the United States.

"Subsection (h)—NON-PREEMPTION OF OTHER REMEDIES.— This subsection makes it clear that the act does not preempt non-federal remedies, whether civil or criminal, for dealing with the theft or misapplication of trade secrets. In particular, the fact that the Attorney General is authorized (under subsection (f) of section 670) to commence civil proceedings in order to enjoin further conduct which would violate section 670 is not to be interpreted to mean that other persons and entities may not also seek injunctive relief that may be available in other civil actions (using state law tort or contract claims) in order to prevent the further misuse of a trade secret.

"Subsection (i)—EXCEPTIONS TO PROHIBITION.—The Act does not prohibit, and is not to be deemed to impair, any otherwise lawful activity conducted by an agency or instrumentality of the United States, a State, or political subdivision of a State. This subsection is intended to make it clear that the act does not prohibit any lawfully authorized investigative, protective, or intelligence activity by one of those government entities. This subsection also makes it clear that it is not a violation of section 670 to report suspected criminal activity to a law enforcement agency or instrumentality of the United States, a State, or political subdivision of a State, to any intelligence agency of the United States, or to Congress.

"Section 3. WIRE AND ELECTRONIC COMMUNICATIONS INTERCEPTION AND INTERCEPTION OF ORAL COMMUNICATIONS.—

This section adds new section 670 to the list of offenses which may be investigated through the use of authorized, wire, oral, or electronic intercepts. This section does not alter the existing standard or procedures for obtaining the authorization to conduct such intercepts."

NOTES

1. Copyright the National Conference of Commissioners on Uniform State Laws. Reprinted here with the express written consent of the National Conference of Commissioners on Uniform State Laws. They may not be reproduced or otherwise duplicated without their express written consent. Some historical materials have been removed, and the text of the act has been modified to eliminate earlier drafts and editorial actions.

2. For clarity, the 1985 amendments have been incorporated into the text.

3. These are the official comments of the drafting committees.

4. U.S. House of Representatives, H. Rep. 104-788, "Economic Espionage Act of 1996," 104th Congress, 2d Session, September 16, 1996, pp. 15–17.

5. The bill discussed by this analysis was later amended during the legislative process. That is the reason for the reference to Sec. 670 et seq., when the law was eventually codified as Sec. 1831 et seq.

C

Organizations Involved with Aspects of Cloaking

COMPETITIVE INTELLIGENCE

Society of Competitive Intelligence Professionals
1700 Diagonal Road #520
Alexandra, VA 22314
Tel.: 703–739–0696. Fax: 703–739–2524.
E-mail: postmaster@scip.org WWW: http://www.scip.org

GOVERNMENT INFORMATION

Open Source Solutions, Inc.
11005 Langton Arms Court
Oakton VA 22124–1807
Tel.: 703–242–1700. Fax: 242–1711. E-mail: oss@oss.net

INDUSTRIAL SECURITY

American Society for Industrial Security
1655 North Fort Meyer Drive
Arlington, VA 22209
Tel.: 703–522–5800. Fax: 703–243–4954.

Glossary

Accuracy The correctness of the particular piece of data you have. You are estimating how correct the data are, based on factors such as whether the data are confirmed by data from a reliable source as well as the reliability of the original source of the data.

Anomaly Data that do not fit; usually an indication that one's working assumptions are wrong or that an unknown factor is affecting results.

Assessment A less formal means of measuring and reporting than an audit.

Audit Independent, structured, and documented evaluation of the adequacy and implementation of an activity to specified requirements. It may examine any element of management control, such as financial, environmental, and quality aspects.

BI Business intelligence.

Blowback The contamination of your own intelligence channels or information by disinformation or misinformation that you have directed at your adversary. In the business context, it means being misled by your own disinformation.

Business Intelligence (BI) One synonym for competitive intelligence.

CI Competitive intelligence or competitive information.

CI Audit A review of your current operations to determine what you actually know about your current competitors and about their operations. A CI audit also helps you focus on what kind of CI you currently need.

CI Cycle The process of establishing CI needs, collecting raw data, processing these data into finished CI, and distributing it to the end-users.

Cloaking Protecting competitively sensitive information from the CI gathering and analytical efforts of competitors.

Competitive Information The result of competitive intelligence.

Competitive Intelligence (CI) The use of public sources to locate and develop data that are then transformed into information, generally about competitors and/or the competition.

Competitive Scenario An analysis of what one or more competitors can be expected to do in response to changes in market and other conditions affecting their activities. The analysis is based on a profile of the competitor, including estimations of its intentions and capabilities stemming from a study of its past actions, and of the perceptions, style, and behavior of its present and future management. Each competitor's actions are studied against the same set of expected market conditions and changes.

Corporate Security The process aimed primarily at protecting and preserving all corporate assets, both tangible and intangible. Typically it operates to set up protections (such as of databases or automobiles), to determine potential threats, and to provide a barrier. In some corporate security operations, a special focus is on the identification and protection of trade secrets. This is also one of the units (IT or IS being the others) involved with "hacking."

Counterintelligence This entails identifying and then foiling a specific competitor's intelligence activities aimed at your firm. It can be styled as "defending against intelligence."

Current Data Facts that deal with a relatively short period of time, centered on the present. Examples of this might be sales figures for the past three-month period for one competitor.

Customer A person or organization, internal or external, which receives or uses outputs from one group or division. These outputs may be products, services, or information.

Data Raw, unevaluated material. Data may be numeric or textual. Data are the ultimate source of information, but become usable information only after the data have been processed and analyzed. See also Current Data, Historic Data, Macro-level Data, and Micro-level Data.

Database Systematically organized data, stored in a computer-readable form so that it can be updated, searched, and retrieved.

Data Mining The process of sifting through massive amounts of data (in computer-readable form) to reveal intelligence, hidden trends, and relationships, usually between customers and products.

Data Warehousing The ability to store large amounts of data by specific categories, so that the data can easily be retrieved, interpreted, and sorted (Data Mining) to provide useful information, typically about customers and products.

Defensive CI (DI) The process of monitoring and analyzing your own business's activities as your competitors and other outsiders see them.

Defensive Intelligence When a firm seeks to find out what its competitors already know and are finding about it through competitive, strategic, and market intelligence activities. Its findings may impact the activities of a corporate security operation, or even corporate counterintelligence.

DI Defensive CI.

Disinformation Incomplete or inaccurate information designed to mislead others about your intentions or abilities. When used in the arena of international politics, espionage, or intelligence, the term means the deliberate production and dissemination of falsehoods, fabrications, and forgeries aimed at misleading an opponent or those supporting an opponent.

Economic Espionage Act of 1996 (EEA) A federal statue, Public Law 104-294 of Oct. 11, 1996, which criminalizes, at the federal level, the misappropriation of trade secrets. It provides additional penalties if such misappropriation is conducted by foreign entities.

EEA Economic Espionage Act of 1996.

E-mail Electronic messaging system.

End-Users Persons or organizations who request and use information obtained from an on-line search or other source of CI.

Espionage Either the collection of information by illegal means or the illegal collection of information. If the information has been collected from a government, this is a serious crime, such as treason. If it is from a business, it may be a theft offense.

False Confirmation A data-verification situation in which a second source of data appears to confirm the data from the first source but does not actually do so. Typically, this arises when the second source receives information from the first source, or both sources receive their data from another common source. They confirm each other not because both are correct, but because both have the same origin.

False Negative When a test gives an erroneous negative result instead of the correct positive result. The result is an erroneous indication that the condition being tested for is not present when it is in fact present.

False Positive When a test gives an erroneous positive result instead of the correct negative result. The result is an erroneous indication that the condition being tested for is present when it is not in fact present.

Firewall A system, often combining both hardware and software, designed to keep outsiders from having access to company computers and databases.

FOIA Freedom of Information Act. See Freedom of Information Act (FOIA).

Fraud An act that involves distributing erroneous or false information with an intent to mislead or take advantage of someone relying on that information.

Freedom of Information Act (FOIA) Federal statute requiring that U.S. government agencies provide information to the public on request. Some agencies make no charge for producing information requested under the FOIA. Others may charge for the time involved as well as the cost of copying the files. Not every federal government record is subject to public disclosure under the FOIA. Important exceptions from disclosure include classified information, personnel files, and some material from private persons and companies that was given to the government but is confidential or proprietary in nature.

Half-Life The period of time for which the raw data you have collected retain at least 50 percent of accuracy and/or relevance.

Historic Data Data that cover a long period of time. These data are designed to show long-term trends, such as gross sales in an industry over a five-year period. This may include projections made covering a long period of years.

Host A computer with full two-way access to other computers on the Internet.

Hypertext A link between one document and other related documents elsewhere in a collection. By clicking on a word (or on a phrase) that has been highlighted by the creator of the document, a user can skip directly to files related to that subject. It can also provide a link to other hosts.

Inductive Methods Problem-solving methods that involve reasoning from particular facts or individual cases to a general conclusion.

Information The material resulting from analyzing and evaluating raw data, reflecting both data and judgments. Information is an input to a finished CI evaluation.

Information Broker A person involved in obtaining data on many subjects, including businesses, from public sources. The sources relied on are exclusively or predominantly public on-line databases. The data are provided without significant screening or analysis. The term originated because such businesses were seen as "brokering" the raw data found in on-line databases by extracting and reselling the data to people who did not use these databases themselves.

Intelligence Knowledge achieved by a logical analysis and integration of available information data on competitors or the competitive environment.

Internet A worldwide computer network, linking host computers and accessible from personal computers. It is also used to mean all forms of electronic communications, such as e-mail, and public hosts, such as America On-Line, which can be accessed through the Internet.

IS Information systems.

IT Information technology.

Japan External Trade Organization (JETRO) An agency of the Japanese government, widely believed to be conducting CI on behalf of the government and Japanese firms.

Macro-Level Data Data of a high level of aggregation, such as the size of a particular market or the overall rate of growth of the nation's economy.

Marketing Intelligence (MI) Intelligence stressing data on pricing, terms, promotions, and their effectiveness.

MI Marketing intelligence.

Micro-Level Data Data of a low level of aggregation or even unaggregated data. This might be data, for example, on a competitor company's or division's sales of a particular product line.

Net The Internet.

On-line Database A computerized database that can be accessed from another computer and through which searches can be conducted from that computer. Typically, this communication occurs over telephone lines.

On-line Searching Using a computer to locate specific information from an on-line database.

Open Source Intelligence (OSCINT) Intelligence developed from nonconfidential, nonproprietary sources only.

Public Relations (PR) In business, this generally refers to the information released to the public by the business through the news media or in speeches. It can also refer to the office or firm responsible for releasing that information.

Reverse Engineering Purchasing and then dismantling a product (or deconstructing a service) to identify how it was designed and constructed. This process enables an investigator to estimate costs and evaluate the quality of the product (or service). In the case of nonpatentable processes and devices, it can also provide information on how to produce a competitive, compatible, or substitute product.

SBU Strategic Business Unit.

Search Statement A description of the specific kinds of data you seek to get from an on-line database. For example, you are seeking information on Golden Bridle Research and you are interested in its activities, if any, in 1990, in the area of CI. Your search statement might ask for documents containing all of the following concepts: Golden Bridle Research and CI (or competitive intelligence) and the year 1996. You would then convert the search into a form that the database could use, using that database's particular protocols.

Securities and Exchange Commission (SEC) An independent agency of the U.S. government.

SI Strategic intelligence.

Society of Competitive Intelligence Professionals (SCIP) The professional society for CI consultants and practitioners.

Stealth Competitor A company which uses cloaking to position itself to compete more effectively.

Strategic Business Unit (SBU) One of several operating entities making up an enterprise.

Strategic Intelligence (SI) Intelligence provided in support of strategic decision making. In the business context, this means providing the highest levels of management information on the competitive, economic, and political environment in which the enterprise operates now and in which it will operate in the future.

Supplier A company or person which provides inputs to tasks or jobs, whether inside or outside of the company.

Surveillance A continuous and systematic watch over the actions of a competitor aimed at providing timely information for immediate responses the competitor's actions.

Target A specified competitor or one of its facilities, activities, or markets.

Trade Secret Protection This is the use of agreements, civil litigation, and even criminal prosecution, under state and federal law, to prevent trade secrets from being used by competitors. Trade secrets are a very narrowly defined type of information. For example, trade-secret protection is available only if the firm treats specific information differently from all other information, and may be lost if the information becomes public, even if by accident.

UCC Uniform Commercial Code.

Uniform Commercial Code (UCC) State law governing, among other things, the filings required by lenders to protect themselves when they make loans to businesses.

Uniform Trade Secrets Act (UTSA) A model law, drafted by the National Conference of Commissioners on Uniform State Laws, dealing with the civil penalties for misappropriation of trade secrets. Last amended in 1985, it has been passed, in one form or another, in forty-one states.

UTSA Uniform Trade Secrets Act.

Video News Releases (VNR) Short video clips provided to television news departments for use on broadcasts.

World Wide Web (WWW) A system for organizing information on the Internet, utilizing hypertext links. By pointing to a highlighted word or phrase and then clicking, a user can move from one Web site to another.

WWW World Wide Web.

Bibliography

COMPETITIVE INTELLIGENCE

Kahaner, Larry. *Competitive Intelligence: From Black Ops to Boardrooms—How Businesses Gather, Analyze, and Use Information to Succeed in the Global Marketplace.* New York: Simon & Schuster, 1996.

McGonagle, John J., and Carolyn M. Vella. *A New Archetype for Competitive Intelligence.* Westport, Conn.: Quorum Books, 1996.

CORPORATE SECURITY

Alster, Norm. "The Valley of the Spies." *Forbes,* 26 October 1992, 200, 201, 204.

The Conference Board, Inc. *Competitive Intelligence* (Research Report No. 913). New York: The Conference Board, Inc., 1988.

DeGenaro, Bill. "Counterintelligence." In *The Art and Science of Business Intelligence Analysis: Intelligence Analysis and Its Applications,* edited by Ben Gilad and Jan P. Herring. Greenwich, Conn.: JAI Press, 1996.

Eels, Richard, and Peter Nehemkis. *Corporate Intelligence and Espionage.* New York: Macmillan, 1984.

Fialka, John J. *War by Other Means: Economic Espionage in America.* New York: W. W. Norton, 1997.

Flanagan, William G., and Brigid McMenamin. "The Playground Bullies Are Learning How to Type." *Forbes,* 21 December 1992, 184–189.

"Guard Your Garbage." *Fortune,* 3 September 1984, 9.

Miles, Gregory. "Information Thieves Are Now Corporate Enemy No. 1." *Business Week,* 5 May 1986, 120–121, 123, 125.

U.S. House Committee on the Judiciary. *The Threat of Foreign Economic Espionage to U.S. Corporations: Hearings before the Subcommittee on Economic and Commercial Law,* 102nd Cong., 2nd Sess., 29 April and 7 May 1992.

Washington Researchers Ltd. *How Competitors Learn Your Company's Secrets.* 2d ed. Washington, D.C.: Washington Researchers Ltd., 1996.

"Weak Links." *InformationWeek,* 10 August 1992, 26–27, 30–31.

Wilder, Clinton, and Bob Violino. "Online Theft." *InformationWeek,* 28 August 1995, 30–40.

Winkler, Ira. *Corporate Espionage.* Rocklin, Calif.: Prima, 1997.

INTELLECTUAL PROPERTY PROTECTION

Elias, Stephen, and Lisa Goldoftas. *Patent, Copyright and Trademark: A Desk Reference on Intellectual Property Law.* Occidental, Calif.: Nolo Press, 1996.

Foster, Frank H., and Robert L. Shook. *Patents, Copyrights & Trademarks.* New York: John Wiley & Sons, 1993.

LEGAL AND ETHICAL ISSUES

Branscomb, Anne Wells. *Who Owns Information? From Privacy to Public Access.* New York: Basic Books, 1995.

Clayton, Mark. "The Usually Legal Business of Keeping Tabs on the Competition." *Christian Science Monitor,* 26 October 1987, 16.

Clayton, Mark. "When Gumshoes Go Too Far." *Christian Science Monitor,* 28 October 1987, 12.

Dorr, Robert C., and Christopher H. Munch. *Protecting Trade Secrets, Patents, Copyright, and Trademarks.* 2d ed. New York: Wiley Law Publications, 1995.

"Ethical Issues in Information-Finding Activities." *The Information Advisor,* February 1989, 1–2.

Lesser, Harry, Ann Lederer, and Charles Steinberg. "Increasing Pressures for Confidentiality Agreements That Work." *Mergers & Acquisitions,* March/April 1992, 23–27.

Lieberstein, Stanley H. *Who Owns What Is in Your Head? A Guide for Entrepreneurs, Inventors and Creative Employees.* Beverly Hills, Calif.: Wildcat Publications, 1996.

TRADE-SECRET PROTECTION

Budden, Michael Craig. *Protecting Trade Secrets under the Uniform Trade Secrets Act.* Westport, Conn.: Greenwood, 1996.

Smith, H. Jefferson. "Yours, Mine and Ours." *Beyond Computing,* November 1995, 12–13.

Weckstein, Kenneth B., and Sandra J. Boyd. "How to Obtain Competitors' Intelligence Legally . . . and How to Protect Your Own." In *Global Perspectives on Competitive Intelligence*, edited by John E. Prescott and Patrick T. Gibbons. Alexandria, Va.: Society of Competitive Intelligence Professionals, 1993.

"When a Rival's Trade Secret Crosses Your Desk." *Business Week*, 20 May 1991, 48.

ANALYSIS

In General

Belkine, Michael. "Intelligence Analysis as Part of Collection and Reporting." In *The Art and Science of Business Intelligence Analysis: Intelligence Analysis and Its Applications*, edited by Ben Gilad and Jan P. Herring, 151–164. Greenwich, Conn.: JAI Press, 1996.

Crossen, Cynthia. *Tainted Truth*. New York: Touchstone, 1996.

Harkleroad, David, and Ken Sawka. "Outthinking the Competition: Intelligence for Strategic Planning." In *The Art and Science of Business Intelligence Analysis: Business Intelligence Theory, Principles, and Uses*, edited by Ben Gilad and Jan P. Herring, 137–157. Greenwich, Conn.: JAI Press, 1996.

Hooper, Todd L., and Linda S. Scott. "Bull's Eye: Taking Aim with Targeted Competitive Assessments." In *The Art and Science of Business Intelligence Analysis: Intelligence Analysis and Its Applications*, edited by Ben Gilad and Jan P. Herring, 53–93. Greenwich, Conn.: JAI Press, 1996.

Osborn, Alex F. *Applied Imagination*. 3d rev. ed. New York: Creative Education Foundation, 1993.

Charting/Mapping

Mathey, Charles. "Competitive Analysis Mapping." *Competitive Intelligence Review*, Fall 1990, 16–17.

Tuohy, Jim. "Tools and Techniques: The Marketplace Environment Map." *Competitive Intelligence Review*, Fall 1990, 34–35.

Yavas, Ugur, and Dogan Eroglu. "Assessing Competitive Edge: Exposition and Illustration of a Diagnostic Tool." *Journal of Consumer Marketing* 12(1996): 47–59.

Content Analysis/Textual Analysis

Achard, P. "Tools and Techniques: The Annual Report—A Legal Document that You Should Read at Regular Intervals." *Competitive Intelligence Review*, Spring 1996, 78–82.

Becker, John. "Supplier Benchmarking." *Competitive Intelligence Review*, Summer 1990, 19–20.

Fahey, Liam. "Understanding Your Competitors' Assumptions." In *Advances in Competitive Intelligence*, edited by John E. Prescott, 71–80. Vienna, Va.: Society of Competitive Intelligence Professionals, 1989.

Fuld, Leonard. "The Moment of Change: Knowing When to Analyze." *Competitive Intelligence Review*, Winter 1994, 32–37.

Kahaner, Larry. "What You Can Learn from Your Competitor's Mission Statements." *Competitive Intelligence Review*, Winter 1995, 35–40.

Kostoff, Ronald N. "Database Tomography for Technical Intelligence." *Competitive Intelligence Review*, Spring 1993, 38–43.

Kostoff, Ronald N. "Database Tomography: Origins and Applications." *Competitive Intelligence Review*, Fall 1990, 48–55.

Paulos, John Allen. *A Mathematician Reads the Newspaper*. New York: Basic Books, 1995.

Press, Gil. "Assessing Competitors' Business Philosophies." *Long Range Planning*, October 1990, 71–75.

Pring, David C. "Competitive Intelligence and Market Research: Filling the Gaps." In *Global Perspectives on Competitive Intelligence*, edited by John E. Prescott and Patrick T. Gibbons, 223–242. Alexandria, Va.: Society of Competitive Intelligence Professionals, 1993.

Stott, Mark D. "Making Sense of the Business Press." *Competitive Intelligence Review*, 1996, S75–S78.

Zahra, Shaker A., and Sherry S. Chaples. "Blind Spots in Competitive Analysis." *Academy of Management Executive*, May 1993, 7–28.

Costs/Financials

Fifer, Robert. "Cost Benchmarking Functions on the Value Chain." *Planning Review*, May/June 1989, 18–23.

Harkleroad, David. "Intelligence Insights from Component Cash Flow." *Competitive Intelligence Review*, Fall 1991, 11–13.

Harkleroad, David. "Sustainable Growth Rate Analysis: Evaluating Worldwide Competitor's Ability to Grow Profitably." *Competitive Intelligence Review*, Summer/Fall 1993, 46–50.

Jacobi, Gary. "Financial Tools for Competitive Analysis." *Competitive Intelligence Review*, Summer 1993, 14–18.

Leonard, James. "Can Actionable Information Be Created from this Mountain of Data? Forecasting Competitors' Strategies from Financial Information." In *Advances in Competitive Intelligence*, edited by John E. Prescott, 151–165. Vienna, Va.: Society of Competitive Intelligence Professionals, 1989.

Mintz, S. L. "The Fraud Detectives." *CFO*, April 1993, 28–33.

Forecasting

Fulmer, Robert M., and Solange Perret. "The Merlin Exercise: Future by Forecast or Future by Invention?" *Journal of Management Development* 12(1993): 44–52.

Sellery, Stephen B. "Forecasting Competitive Pricing." In *Global Perspectives on Competitive Intelligence*, edited by John E. Prescott and Patrick T. Gibbons, 197–204. Alexandria, Va.: Society of Competitive Intelligence Professionals, 1993.

Wang, Clement K., and Paul D. Guild. "Backcasting as a Tool in Competitive Analysis." In *The Art and Science of Business Intelligence: Business Intelligence Theory, Principles, Practices and Uses*, edited by Ben Gilad and Jan P. Herring, 181–198. Greenwich, Conn.: JAI Press, 1996.

Modeling/Scenarios/Shadowing/War Gaming

Berlage, Karsten, and Markus Sulzberger. "Competitive Intelligence and Benchmarking in Practice: A Valuable Management Information Instrument for a Global Universal Bank." In *The Art and Science of Business Intelligence Analysis: Intelligence Analysis and Its Applications*, edited by Ben Gilad and Jan P. Herring, 107–126. Greenwich, Conn.: JAI Press, 1996.

Ellis, R. Jeffrey. "Competitor Scenarios: Extending Scenario Thinking to Competitor Intelligence." In *Advances in Competitive Intelligence*, edited by John E. Prescott, 105–119. Vienna, Va.: Society of Competitive Intelligence Professionals, 1989.

Ellis, R. Jeffrey. "Proactive Competitive Intelligence: Using Competitor Scenarios to Exploit New Opportunities." *Competitive Intelligence Review*, Spring 1993, 13–24.

Harkleroad, David. "Competitor Response Modeling: Out-thinking the Competition." *Competitive Intelligence Review*, 1996, S111–S114.

Himelfarb, Daniel. "Peergroup Baseline Assessment: A Tool for Planning, Corporate Development, and Competitive Analysis." In *Global Perspectives on Competitive Intelligence*, edited by John E. Prescott and Patrick T. Gibbons, 177–188. Alexandria, Va.: Society of Competitive Intelligence Professionals, 1993.

Kesting, William Roy, and Kathleen K. Woods. "Experimental Modeling: Innovation Opportunity for Competitive Intelligence Professionals." *Competitive Intelligence Review*, Winter 1996, 57–68.

Page, Anthony M. "Providing Effective Early Warning: Business Intelligence as a Strategic Control System." In *The Art and Science of Business Intelligence Analysis: Intelligence Analysis and Its Applications*, edited by Ben Gilad and Jan P. Herring, 5–31. Greenwich, Conn.: JAI Press, 1996.

Paul, Pallah, and Dipankar Chakravarti. "Market Structure Analysis Using Managerial Judgments: A Framework and an Experimental Test." *Competitive Intelligence Review*, Winter 1996, 46–56.

Wolters, Karen. "Tools & Techniques: A CI Tool for the 1990s—Red Team/ Blue Team." *Competitive Intelligence Review*, Summer 1994, 51–52.

On-line Sources/Internet

Calof, Jonathan L. "Tools and Techniques: Home Pages—They're Saying More than You Think." *Competitive Intelligence Review*, Winter 1996, 84–85.

Hauser, Rick. "A Structured Process for Collecting, Integrating, and Analyzing Unstructured 'Open Source' Global Strategic Information." *Competitive Intelligence Review*, Fall 1995, 29–34.

Patents/Technology

Ashton, W. Bradford. "An Overview of Business Intelligence Analysis for Science and Technology." In *The Art and Science of Business Intelligence Analysis: Business Intelligence Theory, Principles and Uses*, edited by Ben Gilad and Jan P. Herring, 245–293. Greenwich, Conn.: JAI Press, 1996.

Bigwood, Michael P. "'Normalized' Patent Trend Analysis: Eliminating the Impact of Nonrelevant Variables." *Competitive Intelligence Review*, Winter 1996, 37–45.

Cantrell, Robert. "Tools and Techniques: Patent Intelligence—Information to Compete before Products Are Launched." *Competitive Intelligence Review*, Spring 1996, 65–69.

Klavans, Richard, and Len Simon. "Assessing Competitive R&D Capabilities." *Competitive Intelligence Review*, Fall 1990, 21, 26.

Mogee, Mary Ellen. "Patent Analysis for Strategic Advantage." *Competitive Intelligence Review*, Spring 1994, 27–35.

Zenter, Gene D. "Patent Strategic Analysis of Competitor Research." In *Global Perspectives on Competitive Intelligence*, edited by John E. Prescott and Patrick T. Gibbons, 212–222. Alexandria, Va.: Society of Competitive Intelligence Professionals, 1993.

Using Other Disciplines and Technology

Aiken, Milam, Delvin Hawley, and John Seydel. "Tools and Techniques: Competitive Intelligence through Group Decision Support Systems." *Competitive Intelligence Review*, Summer 1995, 62–66.

Andersen, Sven. "Tools and Techniques: Market Analysis by Means of Trade Statistics." *Competitive Intelligence Review*, Summer 1995, 74–75.

Chen, Ming-Jer. "Competitive Analysis and Inter-Firm Rivalry: Toward a Theoretical Integration." *Academy of Management Journal—Best Papers Proceedings 1995*, 7–11.

Fleisher, Craig. "The Competitive Analysis of Non-Market Intelligence." *Competitive Intelligence Review*, Fall 1990, 11–13.

Mena, Jesus. "Machine-Learning the Business: Using Data Mining for Competitive Intelligence." *Competitive Intelligence Review*, Winter 1996, 18–25.

"Mining for Data." *InformationWeek*, 22 November 1993, 26–31.

"Sales Sleuths Find Solutions." *InformationWeek*, 22 July 1996, 51–52.

Small, Robert D. "Debunking Data-Mining Myths." *InformationWeek*, 20 January 1997, 55–60.

Stotter, James. "Applying Economics to Competitive Intelligence." *Competitive Intelligence Review*, Winter 1996, 26–36.

Index

ABOUT THE AUTHORS

JOHN J. McGONAGLE is Managing Partner of The Helicon Group and CAROLYN M. VELLA is Helicon's Founding Partner. Together they have written five books and dozens of articles on CI and related topics. Internationally recognized for their workshops and seminars, they have advised clients on competitive intelligence and related subjects in Europe, Asia, Australia, and North and South America. Their three other Quorum books are *A New Archetype for Competitive Intelligence* (1996), *Improved Business Planning Using Competitive Intelligence* (1988), and *Competitive Intelligence in the Computer Age* (1987).